A Computer Simulation of Democratic Political Development:
Tests of the Lipset and Moore Models

ROLAND F. MOY
Department of Political Science
APPALACHIAN STATE UNIVERSITY
(BOONE, NORTH CAROLINA)

SAGE PUBLICATIONS / Beverly Hills   London

Copyright © 1971 by Sage Publications, Inc.

Printed in the United States of America

All rights reserved. No part of this book may be reproduced or utilized in any form or by any means, electronic or mechanical, including photocopying, recording, or by any information storage and retrieval system, without permission in writing from the publisher.

For information address:

SAGE PUBLICATIONS, INC.
275 South Beverly Drive
Beverly Hills, California 90212

SAGE PUBLICATIONS, INC.
St George's House / 44 Hatton Garden
London E C 1

International Standard Book Number 0-8039-0162-3

Library of Congress Catalog Card No. 72-172473

FIRST PRINTING

CONTENTS

INTRODUCTION 5
    Development and Democracy 5
    Using Simulation in Research 7

A MODEL OF LIPSET'S THEORY 11
    Overview of Theory Propositions 11
    Branch Point Variables and Assumptions 14

A MODEL OF MOORE'S THEORY 24
    Overview of Theory Propositions 24
    Branch Point Variables and Assumptions 30

ANALYSIS OF MOORE MODEL DATA 35

ANALYSIS OF LIPSET MODEL DATA 43

SUMMARY AND IMPLICATIONS 52

APPENDICES 57

NOTES 67

REFERENCES 70

LIST OF TABLES AND FIGURES

Figure 1	Value Pattern Variable Scales	16
Figure 2	Value Variability Limitation	17
Figure 3	Identity of Agents and Source of Authority Formula	23
Figure 4	Acceptance of Democratic Principles Formula	23
Table 1	Correlations Between Dependent Measures	36
Table 2	Manova Tests of Significance Using Wilks Lambda Criterion	37
Table 3	Univariate Anova F Tests	37
Table 4	Manova-Related Tests	38
Table 5	Manova Test of Significance Using Wilks Lambda Criterion for AB Interaction	40
Table 6	Univariate Anova F Tests of AB Interaction Effects	40
Table 7	Marginal Means	41
Table 8	Scheffé Test on A and B	42
Table 9	Correlations Between Dependent Variables	44
Table 10	Manova Tests of Significance Using Wilks Lambda Criterion	45
Table 11	Univariate Anova F Tests	45
Table 12	Manova-Related Tests	46
Table 13	Manova Tests of Significance for Interaction Using Wilks Lambda Criterion	47
Table 14	Univariate Anova F Tests for Interaction	48
Table 15	Marginal Means—Lipset Model	50
Table 16	Scheffé Test on A, B, and C	50

A Computer Simulation of Democratic Political Development: Tests of the Lipset and Moore Models

ROLAND F. MOY
Appalachian State University

INTRODUCTION

DEVELOPMENT AND DEMOCRACY

Since the time of the French and American Revolutions, there has been support for the idea that there is a natural tendency to evolve toward what is now called a democratic form of government (Mill, 1958: ch. 18; MacIver, 1926: 340; 1947: 174, 188-192; Lerner 1958: 60-61). Other writers have held similar views and have attempted to delineate the cultural, social, and economic patterns which a society must possess as it moves toward stable democratic government (Shils, 1965: 7-10; Emerson, 1964: 221, 292; Lipset, 1960: 27-86; Cutright, 1963). They have attempted to establish the necessary, if not sufficient, preconditions for democracy.

In a reaction to some of these conceptions of political modernization, another approach has developed which does not concern itself with

---

AUTHOR'S NOTE: *This is a revised and expanded version of a paper delivered at the Sixty-Sixth Annual Meeting of the American Political Science Association, September 1970. It was prepared with the assistance of Professor Philip M. Burgess and Lawrence S. Mayer of the Behavioral Sciences Laboratory, The Ohio State University, and with the facilities of The Ohio State University Computer Center.*

development toward democracy as a focus of concern. In attempting to explain political change, the stress is upon the factors which contribute to development toward stable and effective government, regardless of its democratic character (Huntington, 1965: 386-430; Field, 1967; Almond and Powell, 1966). A somewhat similar viewpoint, which is not directly concerned with the development toward democracy or with the establishment of a stable or institutionalized political system at any particular level of modernization, is advanced by those writers who examine the general processes of change and the patterns which such change takes as a society evolves over time (Deutsch, 1961; Eisenstadt, 1964, 1966). Usually it is assumed that change toward greater complexity and diversity is part of a worldwide trend, and it is not posited that this process will necessarily move toward what we consider a democratic form of government, but that it is only a possibility.

Differing from those who consider development toward democracy a necessary outgrowth of economic and social change and diversification, and beyond those who examine political and social development without any consideration of democratic development, there are writers who consider that the development of democratic government will be desirable and useful (but not necessary) for dealing with the complexity and diversity which modernization brings (Pye, 1964: 301, 1966: 80, 81, 87; Apter, 1965: 38, 483). According to this view, if democratic government is not a necessary outcome, it is deemed to have a high probability of becoming established, given a certain level of modernization and the guidance of enlightened elites.

This brief review of political development and modernization frameworks and propositions illustrates that there has been a continuing interest in the development of political democracy, and that a clear distinction can be made between patterns of development toward political effectiveness and stability, and development toward political democracy. Seymour Lipset (1963: 36) and Barrington Moore (1966: 414, 467, 468) also note this distinction and direct their efforts toward explaining the latter process. Both writers have produced a book-length analysis of the factors they feel are important for the development of conditions for democratic government. These analyses are focused more narrowly on the development of democracy than other recent studies of modernization which may include some discussion of democracy (such as those by Lerner, Pye, Apter, and Emerson cited above), and they present a longitudinal and more extensive analysis of conditions for democracy than those presented recently by people such as Cutright (1963) and Neubauer (1967). Although the works are extended on the problem of democratic development, neither writer presents a comprehensive theory. Both focus on a few key variables or factors in an attempt to gain conceptual clarity and analytic focus while explaining a rather broad-scale phenomenon. Because of these considerations, and because the theory-building effort is inductive rather than deductive, however, the narrowed focus appears justified (Meehan, 1965: 152, 515).

The two writers differ in focus and in variables used in explanation of the process under analysis. Moore is primarily concerned with the patterns of social and economic change (especially the landlord-peasant relationship) which produce the conditions (or preconditions) under which a democratic form of government can emerge.[1] He implies that these conditions, if present at its inception, will tend to enable the democratic system to persist (or be stable). Lipset, on the other hand, is primarily concerned with patterns of values and system performance which enable a newly established democracy (primarily democratic in form) to persist and remain viable (stable, and democratic in content or operation as well as in form).[2] These two analyses of democratic political development, therefore, represent different, yet not entirely alternative or competitive approaches to the similar problem of specifying, from their representative points of view, some key necessary conditions for stable democratic government. They are different in terms of the explanatory factors utilized and in historical focus. Although Moore implies that the conditions he specifies are relevant to the newly formalized democratic system, the difference in explicit focus opens the possibility that they may be complementary and not entirely competing or contradictory explanations, in the sense that the economic and social conditions (of Moore's analysis) which precede the founding of a democratic state may be useful or necessary to produce the values (of Lipset's analysis) which sustain it after its inception.

The examination of the relationship of these two theories, as well as of their individual validity, are matters for empirical testing. To facilitate such an examination, a computer simulation model of each theory was developed. The data generated by the simulation runs were subjected to statistical tests which explicate in more detail the implications of these two verbal theories by developing propositions of greater specificity which will enable empirical tests to be made as data become available.

USING SIMULATION IN RESEARCH

It might be asked, why simulate? What is the advantage that one might gain using a computer simulation of models of these two theories? It should be noted that both theories to be examined are attempts to explain or illuminate a very complex process—the process of development toward a democratic polity. Because it is a complex process, the theories must examine many variables, and many propositions concerning interactions between variables are advanced. It is true that neither author deals with all the variables involved (Lipset, 1963: 10, 208, 343, 344), but their constructs do involve sufficient complexities and a number of assumptions, some explicit and some implicit, which must be dealt with in a systematic manner to facilitate a more precise understanding and evaluation of the implications of the theories.

Verba (1964: 515) notes that a "simulation adds an important link between theory and the real world. It can be *designed to work as if the theory were correct;* and in this way can generate the implications of the theory." If certain conditions imply certain outcomes, the simulation results will specify these in a way that provides for empirical testing a more detailed array of the hypotheses implicit in the theory.[3] Modeling for simulation purposes also provides another opportunity to specify implications of a theory, not by generating them in the output, but by specifying the necessary assumptions and conditions without which the process could not be realized in the way desired (Frijda, 1967: 60). The verbal theory may sound plausible, but it may leave implicit or unspecified many propositions relating variables which must be made explicit if a model of the theory is to be constructed and made to "work" as intended by the theorist.

In order to carry out a computer simulation, then, it is necessary that the theory (or the propositions comprising the theory) be stated systematically in the form of a model. The model expresses the theory, the referent of which is the external world. A simulation model is not an ideal type, nor does it reproduce every detail of a referent system. Rather, it extracts those factors which are deemed most relevant by the theory and does so explicitly while attempting to ensure that the variables and the relationships included in the model respond in a manner comparable to that of the behavior of the real system as stated by the theory (Dawson, 1962: 3).

A computer simulation offers several advantages in dealing with complex data. Among them are the vividness with which the model delineates the relationships which are important in the operation of the model plus the ability of the model to cope accurately and rapidly with the complexities of a large number of variables in a way that would be most difficult to do without the use of such a model, enabling the analyst to observe the outcomes or consequences of the initial conditions and theoretical propositions, posited by the theory to be tested, which structure the operation of the model. In addition, one has the ability to manipulate the operation of the system in a way that may not be available in the empirical world, thereby gaining insight into processes which an empirical investigation may not be able to uncover (Zelditch and Evans, 1962: 49).

A simulation is especially useful when one wants to study a developmental process, because a computer simulation is an activity or process and not a simple analysis of a static model. It is a study of the interaction of variables over time by observing the behavior of a theory-based model of a referent system which changes as it is posited that the referent would change under similar conditions (Evans et al., 1967: 6).

The two theoretical formulations to be examined rely on data primarily qualitative in nature and designed to be illustrative. As a result, it is very difficult to devise empirical tests of their theories, inasmuch as hard empirical data, especially for the long time span involved, are not readily available and perhaps will not be for some time in the future. There are data archives being developed which offer some possibility that sufficient data will be collected in the near future which will enable a more thorough testing of these and other theories. In the meantime, the relevant step of theory elaboration and specification can be undertaken on the important question of democratic political development. Rather than change the research subject for lack of empirical data, a change in analysis technique is proposed.

The most relevant technique for elaboration and specification appears to be that of using computer simulation of models of the theories to be examined and to use, where necessary, empirically derived propositions to elaborate the theories for the model-building process. Even if the propositions are only tentative, they can fill the gaps in the theoretical knowledge of conditions and of interactions of variables by making explicit assumptions about these conditions and interactions such that a working model can be developed and put into operation for a series of runs in a computer simulation.

It should be noted that the number of assumptions made in computer simulation models does not greatly exceed that made in the course of developing the verbal theories. The assumptions are more obvious, because all of them have to be made explicit in order for the theory to function as an operating model for a simulation. Many factors that verbal theories leave implicit, or assume to be constant factors, have to be explicitly noted and, if necessary, given definite values so that the model functions and generates output that can be traced to certain input variables. In other words, it is a more rigorous explication of verbal theory (Holland and Gillespie, 1963: 206, 207).

A simulation model is useful for dealing with complexity. But a model, if it is to be analyzed adequately, should not be so complex that it is difficult to understand or impossible to trace patterns of variable interaction. The simulation model, therefore, must be complex enough to include the variables to be examined, yet not too complex to prevent adequate analysis. Perhaps a rule of thumb might be that the stronger the theory, the fewer the variables one need use. Conversely, the less adequate the theory the more variables one must consider (Zelditch and Evans, 1962: 52). In the present state of theoretical development in political science, one can argue that the models would have to be rather complex. This does not mean, however, that the model must include all the variables deemed important for a political system, but may, as Lipset does, exclude certain variables and concentrate on others which are most pertinent to the purpose of the research. In Lipset's case, of course, this framework focuses on the impact of prevalent societal values on the operation of the political system. In dealing with a reduced number of variables, the researcher is enabled to set aside a good deal of "noise" that might otherwise distract him (Scott et al., 1966: 70).

The preceding comments about computer simulation are not meant to imply that this analysis technique is a foolproof shortcut to greater knowledge and understanding. There are difficulties to be faced with this approach just as there are with any alternative one may choose. Among these difficulties are at least three of some importance. The first is that one cannot be certain that the assumptions made concerning quantification and scaling of variables and constants are adequate. There is a danger that the resulting model operation will not follow the same behavior characteristics of the modeled theory. Validity checks can be attempted and the judgment and advice of others can be a helpful check on these assumptions.[4] Second, at the analysis stage, there will be no obvious path of causation between input and output. The intervening framework of theoretical propositions is complex. These propositions must, nevertheless, be tested to determine the implications which they have for output, given certain initial conditions.[5] Third, it is not a simple task to compare simulation results with the referent sytem. The empirical world is not conveniently organized in patterns that might be labeled, "low," "medium," or "high." It is assumed, nevertheless, that the development of more specific propositions will facilitate empirical testing.

A MODEL OF LIPSET'S THEORY

OVERVIEW OF THEORY PROPOSITIONS

Lipset's approach to an explanation of democratic political development is not meant to be a comprehensive theory but is intended to demonstrate the independent explanatory power of value analysis in understanding political evolution.[6] Although technological change can affect values over a period of time, they are slow to change. Values become "structured predispositions" which are stable enough to influence the course of political development for generations to come in areas of political relationships, religion, the status system, and the class interests of workers (Lipset, 1963: 7, 123, 207).

In politics, the value patterns operate to condition institutional arrangements and to shape the outcomes of group conflicts so that group members make adjustments to new conditions within the framework of the dominant value system.[7] For Lipset, the major focus of activity in the political realm appears to be the activity of various groups as they try to assert themselves as the economy grows and new social patterns emerge. These groups compete with one another and also seek access to the political system for the advantages which participation in the political system can bring to them in their other activities. As the society develops, the existing distribution of resources and privileges, as well as the legitimacy of the political decision-making process, come under severe tension. The existing elite may adjust either by incorporating the new groups or by insulating themselves from the new rising elite (Lipset, 1963: 239). The first option may offer more possibilities of continued stability for the existing structure of authority, whereas the second tends to result in a polarization of interests and of values resulting in an unstable political situation.

As is noted in the accompanying flow chart (see Appendix A) the pattern of acceptance by the ruling elite of the rising groups as they seek access to the political sphere depends upon the level of tolerance that the elite has for the new groups, the effectiveness of the social and economic systems for the competing groups, and the level of legitimacy which the political system has for these groups. The patterns of legitimacy, tolerance, and effectiveness which characterize the political system will indicate its stability.[8] These patterns, together with certain environmental and value patterns, will determine whether or not progress toward democratic government will also be possible, as the remainder of the flow chart indicates. It illustrates that, as a nation develops toward an increasing acceptance of democratic principles (especially the "rules of the game" for democratic succession to political office), a broader socialization of conflict (broader peaceful participation in the political process) and a reduced identity of the source and agents of authority (greater distinction between legitimating factor and those individuals acting in the name of that factor), the probability of *democracy* becoming stable improves. As Lipset notes, it is these groups in their political activity, together with the established elites, which are the key to democratic development and political stability. These are the elements of society which maintain the value patterns of the society and are the ones whose commitment to democratic principles will determine whether or not the society will remain democratic, even though a broad public adherence to democratic principles is evident.[9] In other words, the organized groups and political elite are keys to stability and democratic political development.

More specifically, as the outcome of the first branch point indicates, the level of effectiveness can have an effect on the level of legitimacy of the system for the group. If effectiveness is sufficient, it will increase the legitimacy of the system, and, if the effectiveness is not sufficient, it will decrease the legitimacy of the system (Lipset, 1963: 45, 60). As the second branch point shows, if the legitimacy of the system based on past experience is too low, the group will attempt to seek its interests outside the established political system and a polarization within the society will occur (Lipset, 1963: 18, 239; 1960: 64, 65). If legitimacy is still sufficient, however, the group will attempt to present its demands through the political system, as indicated by the righthand side of the flow chart. Whether or not the group is successful will depend upon the tolerance of those in political control. The third and fourth branch points indicate that if the ruling elite has sufficient tolerance for the group seeking access, and the threat the group presents is sufficiently weak, the group will be given access. If the group is given access, the tolerance of the threatening group for the political elite will be increased and they will continue to operate within the established political institution (Lipset, 1963: 239, 242, 289). If they are not given access—that is, if the tolerance of the ruling elite is not sufficient or the threat is too much for the ruling elite to accept—then their access demand will be opposed, and the tolerance of the threatening group will be reduced.

It is assumed that if most major groups of the society continue to operate within the system and the tolerance levels remain sufficiently high, the system will remain stable in its operation. Beyond the condition of mere stability, Lipset notes that "one of the necessary conditions for a stable *democratic* polity is a clear distinction between the source of sovereignty and the agents of authority" (Lipset, 1963: 10, 11; italics in original; 313, 314). To operationalize this for the model, it might be assumed, therefore, that if tolerance levels are high enough and a sufficient number of groups are operating within the system, as indicated by the next branch point (no. 5), there will be a tendency toward a reduced identity of (an increased distinction between) the agents of authority and the source of that authority, whether it is a written constitution or an unwritten tradition which legitimates the regime. Conversely, if enough groups are operating outside the established political institutions and the tolerance level is low enough, there will be a tendency for an increased identification of the established elite and their source of authority.

Another part of the democratization process is referred to indirectly by Lipset. It is concerned with the commitment to democratic principles or "rules of the game."[10] Following the implications of this concern, it seems reasonable to elaborate the theory for the purposes of the model by assuming that if conditions for the acceptance of democratic principles are sufficient there will be a possibility for an increase in that commitment if a new elite or a new group or coalition exerts itself and attempts to gain political control (branch points 6 and 7). The conditions assumed to be relevant for this potential are two: that most politically relevant groups, first, are committed to the system and, second, have sufficient tolerance for the system and its policies. Under these conditions, a shift in political control will not be much of a challenge to the basic interests of the relevant groups. Since the peaceful change in power under democratic rules would not be destabilizing, there would appear to be a propensity to increasingly accept those rules as they repeatedly prove functional for peaceful political change. Similarly, if no challenge for power is made, the rules are assumed to have been tacitly functional and a smaller increase in their acceptance is assumed to occur (see Appendix C). If such conditions are not present, on the other hand, such an attempt by a new elite will result in reduction of the acceptance of democratic principles. It is through such experiences that the "rules of the game" of succession to office are developed.

This leads to the next branch point (no. 8), which assumes that the greater the acceptance of democratic principles (see above) and the higher the tolerance levels of both the political elite and competing groups, the greater the probability that further democratization and stability will develop. This possibility arises on the assumption that, on occasion, insoluble problems will confront the decision-making elite. If such an event occurs, there will be a tendency to do one of two things, depending upon the level of the elements noted above. If they are not high enough and an insoluble problem develops, it will tend to result in either a nondemocratic (or nonpeaceful) socialization of conflict or a repression of the challenging groups by the established elite, thereby lowering the legitimacy of the system for the challenging groups. On the other hand, if the levels are high enough and an insoluble problem presents itself, there will tend to be a democratic socialization of conflict to allow a legitimate and more widespread opportunity for other groups, the general public, or the mass media to participate in the resolution of the problem at hand.

The inclusion of such a process in our model appears to be justified by Lipset's concern for both expanding the sphere of influence of public opinion as far as practicable and establishing opposition political parties to make government effectively democratic. Party competition implies that broader publics will choose between them and that there will be adherence to democratic rules of the game if stable democracy is to survive. It also implies that there will be protection of the attendant civil liberties, organized opposition, and rule of law required for a successful operation of such a democratic system (Lipset, 1963: 10, 11, 36, 208, 313, 314, 316, 317). Such a process of socialization of conflict, it would appear, also tends to further the reduction of the identity of the agents and source of authority. This would appear to be true because the tendency to include a wider population in the political process tends to legitimate that activity and tends, therefore, to reduce the legitimacy of the political elites to act on their own authority without the sanction of either popular demand in the electoral process or of popular sovereignty as authorized by a written or unwritten constitution, or both.

The model outputs of legitimacy, tolerance, and number of groups operating within the system would be indicators of the degree of stability of the political system. The model outputs of degree of identity of source of authority and agents of authority, the degree of socialization of conflict, and the degree of acceptance of democratic principles would be indicators of the degree of democratic development. The broader the participation that is possible, the freer the competition between opposing groups in and out of political office, the more representative the elected agents, and the more the people are deemed to be the source of authority for the government, the more democratic a given country may be considered. All the indicators together would be an index, therefore, of the degree of democratic political development.

BRANCH POINT VARIABLES AND ASSUMPTIONS

This section will attempt to spell out in more specific detail the formulae for determining which option will be taken at each branch point of the model and the assumptions concerning group activity and model operation sequences. These statements will make it possible to translate the verbalized model into computer programming language with a minimum of additional conceptualization.

For the purposes of model operation, it is assumed that there are five groups which form the center of activity in the political system. It is further assumed that these five groups will reflect the general pattern of prevailing values of society and, therefore, that all five groups will operate within the context of the value patterns which characterize a society. These five groups do not represent specific politically relevant groups of a given society, but it will be assumed that their behavior patterns in the model will parallel the activity patterns of the groups dealt with by the theory; groups such as the military, the trade unions, business and religious organizations, agricultural interests, and the intellectual elite.

Because of the limitations of present computer operations, these groups will not interact at the same time within the political system, but will operate in a sequential pattern, one group at a time. This is a distortion of reality, but there will still be a cumulative effect registered by their operation as the simulation proceeds, a process which will not be unlike that of the modeled theory. The five groups are also assumed to be roughly equal in terms of political resources and therefore the concentration of a majority or more of them within or without the established institutions will have the stabilizing or destabilizing consequences one might expect. There is a further assumption that it is possible for the established political elite to continue in political control without the necessary support of any one of the groups. Consequently, any combination of groups could presumably make up an effective coalition able to maintain a stable and even democratic government. As an initial condition, each of the five groups will be randomly assigned a tolerance level. As the groups operate within or without the political institutions of the society, the tolerance levels will change and affect, therefore, the future operation of the system.

The patterns of value which shall characterize the model for each computer run shall be determined as initial conditions. Although Lipset (1963: 212, 217 and throughout) deals with value patterns primarily at the national level, he also examines the relevance of differing value patterns in subsystems of the society such as the economy, polity, and social status systems. The primary politically relevant value patterns, however, are those which characterize the economy and the polity (Lipset, 1963: 234, 268). We will, therefore, include in the model only the value patterns for the economy and the polity and not concern ourselves with value patterns of the social status systems.

The patterns of value which shall characterize the model for each computer run shall be determined as initial condition. lthough Lipset (1963: 212,217 and throughout) deals with value patterns primarily at the national level, he also examines the relevance of differing value patterns in subsystems of the society such as the economy, polity, and social status systems. The primary politically relevant value patterns, however, are those which characterize the economy and the polity (Lipset, 1963: 234,268). We will, therefore, include in the model only the value patterns for the economy and the polity and not concern ourselves with value patterns of the social status systems.

The value patterns which Lipset uses in his analysis are the four continua of achievement-ascription, equalitarianism-elitism, universalism-particularism, and specificity-diffuseness.[11] These values can usefully be depicted as varying along 100-point scales for the economy and the polity as indicated in Figure 1.

The amount of variability among the four scales of value patterns is limited by at least three propositions which Lipset advances. Figure 2 illustrates the relationships which he posits between the achievement-ascription continuum and the equalitarianism-elitism continuum. It can be noted that two conditions govern their relationship. The first is that, if equalitarianism is high, achievement will be high; and second, if ascription is high, elitism will be high (Lipset, 1963: 2, 211). A third restraint on variability is that if the achievement-ascription *and* universalism-particularism levels are at either extreme, the equalitarianism-elitism and specificity-diffuseness levels cannot be at the opposite extreme. There is a positive correlation between the two sets of value levels (Lipset: 211, footnote). The precise correlation level, however, is not given.

Economy			Polity		
Ascrip.		Achiev.	Ascrip.		Achiev.
0	50	100	0	50	100
Elit.		Equal.	Elit.		Equal.
0	50	100	0	50	100
Partic.		Univ.	Partic.		Univ.
0	50	100	0	50	100
Diff.		Spec.	Diff.		Spec.
0	50	100	0	50	100

Figure 1: VALUE PATTERN VARIABLE SCALES

Ascrip. 0	Achiev. 100
0 Elit.	↓ ↑ 100 Equal.

The pointers may vary to either extreme, but cannot pass one another.

Figure 2: VALUE VARIABILITY LIMITATION

Lipset analyzes only a few of the possible combinations of economic and political value levels. An analysis of all the possible levels of values and of combinations of values will likewise not be attempted here because of the large number of patterns that could be arranged. For example, even if only three levels [high (90), medium (50), low (10)] are assigned to each of the four values in both the economy and the polity, there would be 48 possible patterns of values for each subsystem (given the restraints on variability noted above). Combining these with only three levels of economic development (discussed below) there would be 48x48x3 or 6,918 possible patterns of initial conditions to be analyzed. To reduce the analysis to manageable proportions while engaging in an examination of a broader spectrum of initial conditions than that which Lipset considers, therefore, it will be necessary to limit both the number of levels and the degree of intrasystem variability. To do this, we will utilize only three levels for the values (90, 50, 10) which will represent most of the spectrum of possible levels. In addition, where necessary (as noted in discussions related to various branch points below), the values of the economy (or polity) will be treated as varying in a manner such that a mean of the four would equal the three levels noted above. In this manner, the number of initial condition patterns to be analyzed (when combined with three levels of economic development) is reduced to 3x3x3 or 27.

The other initial condition that must be established is the speed or rate of economic development which the society is undergoing. Lipset makes several references to the relationship between economic growth and the stability and legitimacy of the system, and these will be noted as we move from branch point to branch point. At this point, however, it can be noted that the rate of economic growth can also be initialized on a 100-point scale. This level can then be related to the prevailing value patterns in the propositions which govern the branch points of the model.

These initial conditions specified for economic values, political values, and economic development will form an essential part of the framework within which the groups must operate as they are brought into contact with the political system. The values of tolerance, effectiveness, and legitimacy will be initialized on a 100-unit scale. At each point in the model that requires a change in level, the change shall be one unit in size unless otherwise noted. Each of the five groups plus elements of the political system, therefore, will have its own scale for ranking the variables relevant to it. The five groups will be scaled on the tolerance variable, while the political system will be scaled on the probability of effectiveness and legitimacy (plus system tolerance as noted below).

We now come to the first branch point of the model, which is that of the effectiveness level. It should be noted again that the effectiveness and legitimacy probability levels are system attributes which affect group action in the system, while tolerance levels are group attributes. All three may change as the model operates, and their cumulative change will shape the pattern of development reflected in the model output.

The crucial variables affecting effectiveness levels of the system are perceptions of opportunities in the economic system and perceptions of the importance of government to those opportunities. If achievement values are high, then awareness of the importance of government to those opportunities will tend to be high (Lipset, 1963: 245). Also, the greater the achievement orientation, the greater the need for opportunities in the economic and social spheres (Lipset, 1963: 246). In other words, a rapidly expanding economy would provide many opportunities for rising groups, and provide the level of effectiveness necessary to maintain stability when achievement values are high. On the other hand, the more rapid the economic development while ascriptive values are high, the greater the difficulty in achieving or maintaining effectiveness (Lipset, 1963: 246). This assumes that people holding achievement values are more open to the changes brought about by rapid economic development.

To operationalize the above propositions concerning effectiveness, the following scheme is utilized. The economic system achievement value is initialized on a 100-point scale (at 90, 50, or 10) and is modified by the rate of growth in the economy to arrive at an initial level of system effectiveness. The modification can be derived as follows. The rate of per capita GNP growth is determined on a 100-point scale to reflect high, medium, and low growth rates (again specified as 90, 50, 10). Although we are modeling the theory which Lipset develops, he does not specify the growth rates he has in mind when speaking of a rapidly expanding economy. Empirically, growth rates appear usually to vary from 0-9% annually.[12] It would not appear unrealistic, therefore, to note that the scaled levels of 90, 50, and 10 for per capita annual growth parallel the empirical pattern of 9, 5, and 1%. We arrive at an effectiveness level for the system by assuming that if the differentiation between the achievement level and the growth rate level exceed 10 points of difference (to allow some margin for error in calculating the effect such a deviation has) then for every point of disparity over 10, whether higher or lower, one shall subtract that amount as a percentage from the achievement level to arrive at the initial effectiveness level.[13] For example, if the achievement level is 75 and the growth rate level is 50, there would be a 15-point disparity beyond the 10-point leeway allowed. Subtracting 15% of the 75 from 75 leaves a total of 66, which would be the initial level of effectiveness. This initial level, once derived from initial conditions, remains constant for the series of computer runs for which it is used. As different initial conditions are posited for different simulation runs, then a new initial effectiveness level is also derived using the same formula for determining that level.

Given the initial effectiveness level, the tolerance level of each group will modify it as the group proceeds to interact within the model. It is assumed that the tolerance level of each group will have an independent effect upon its perceptions of how effective the system may be in providing opportunities to satisfy demands. If there is low tolerance, for example, then, however high the objective level of effectiveness or opportunity may be, it will still be perceived to be lower. The formula for arriving at the effectiveness level for each group, therefore, is proposed as follows. For each point of disparity between the tolerance level and the midpoint of the 100-point tolerance scale, that amount in percentage terms shall be either added to or subtracted from the initial effectiveness level. If the tolerance level is below the midpoint, the amount is subtracted, and, if it is above, that amount shall be added. For example, if the initial effectiveness level is 66 and the group tolerance level is 40, then 10% of the 66 (6.6) is subtracted from 66 leaving a remainder (rounded off) of 59. This level of 59 could then be called the perceived system effectiveness level.

It should be noted that the levels determined at each branch point, whether for effectiveness, legitimacy, elite tolerance, or some other variable of the model, provide a measurement point against which is compared a randomly chosen number which may assume any integer value between 0 and 100. Hence, the option as to which branch point exit is selected is not completely determinative but has a random element which is modified by the changes which develop in tolerance levels and other factors as the model is operated. To illustrate by continuing the above example, if the random number is larger than 59, the effectiveness level is deemed to be not satisfactory and the "no" exit from the effectiveness branch point will be taken. Conversely, if the random number is less than 59, the "yes" option from the effectiveness branch point is selected. As each group passes through the effectiveness branch point there will be a different group effectiveness level and a different random number for comparative purposes. A different possibility exists each time, therefore, as to which exit from the branch point is selected. A similar process occurs at the other branch points of the model.[14]

As was noted in the first major section of this paper, if effectiveness is sufficient, it will tend to increase the legitimacy of the system. It should be noted, however, that it is tenuous to depend upon effectiveness alone to develop legitimacy for the system, because this requires a rapid change toward a high level of economic achievement orientation if they are not already at a high level—a most difficult process (Lipset, 1963: 245, 246, 314). Because of the necessity of having a high economic achievement orientation level to permit system effectiveness to increase system legitimacy, it was assumed in arriving at the initial effectiveness level that low achievement levels would not result in the type of system effectiveness that would tend to increase system legitimacy. In other words, it is necessary to have high achievement levels to result in high effectiveness levels which can produce a payoff of increasing system legitimacy.

As we move to a consideration now of the legitimacy branch point (no. 2), it should be noted that Lipset was dealing with the problem of establishing legitimacy in a new nation; that is, one that has overthrown its traditional pattern of legitimacy and is now attempting to operate within some sort of rational constitutional framework. Consequently, the new regime must prove itself effective in order to maintain itself in the long run as the legitimate government. Lipset advances several propositions concerning the probability of a regime developing long-term legitimacy. One is that if the nation has a high achievement level and a high equalitarianism level, together with a third factor which may be either strong religion, adequate social mobility, or opportunities for satisfaction through political involvement, then the regime has a high probability of attaining or maintaining adequate and long-term legitimacy (Lipset, 1963: 271-273). He also theorizes that, if there are adequate access opportunities for rising groups in the social and economic system, these will also tend to increase legitimacy (Lipset, 1963: 239, 242). Finally, as was indicated previously, he proposes that continued effectiveness will increase the legitimacy of the political system (Lipset, 1963: 45, 46, 60).

With these propositions in mind, we may now attempt to develop a formula for determining the initial probability of legitimacy for the system. The second and third propositions, it should be noted, are accounted for in the establishment of the initial effectiveness level and in the relationship of system effectiveness to system legitimacy. The first proposition appears insufficient as a basis for establishing initial system legitimacy for our model because it attempts to explain a long-term process rather than establish initial conditions, plus the fact that other combinations of values with other factors could also aid legitimacy. This leaves us with the consideration that most new nations generally begin their course of development with rather high legitimacy as a residue of earlier efforts to establish the new regime. We might, therefore, initialize legitimacy at an arbitrary level of 75 and permit the operation of the model to determine whether or not the system is capable of maintaining that level or of improving upon it. As in the previous branch point, a random number is selected to compare with the legitimacy level to determine which exit is taken as the model operates.

At branch point 3 there appear to be three key factors involved in determining the tolerance level of the political elite for the threatening group. The first is stated in the proposition that the stronger the four political values of achievement, equalitarianism, universalism, and specificity, the stronger the tolerance for access demands (Lipset, 1963: 214). The second proposition is that the more the levels of value acceptance are the same in both the economy and in the polity, the greater the tolerance for access demands.[15] The third is that since tolerance is a relationship between political elite and challenging group, it would be reasonable to assume that the tolerance of the group for the system would also affect the relationship. From these propositions, we may derive the probability level of tolerance for the threatening group by the following procedure. Since political values appear to be the crucial factor in determining tolerance for political demands in a developing democracy, the primary factor in determining tolerance levels will be the mean level of the polity values. This initial level will be modified by the degree of discrepancy between that level and the mean of economic system values. The absolute difference between means will be used as a percentage figure to subtract that amount from the polity value level to find a net probability of tolerance level. Then, as each group interacts in the system, its tolerance level will further modify the net level of system tolerance. If group tolerance is above the midpoint (50), the net tolerance level will be increased by a percentage equal to the difference between 50 and the group tolerance level. If group tolerance is below the midpoint, the difference is substracted by the same procedure. Again, as in the previous branch points, a random number will be matched against this level to determine which alternative of the branch point will be selected.

At branch point 4, the size of the threat, three key propositions are involved in determining this level. The first is that the size of the threatened change will tend to be small if the three economic values of equalitarianism, universalism, specificity are strong (Lipset, 1963: 214). The second proposition is that the better the economic opportunities of the system, the less there will tend to be a serious threat to the established elite (Lipset, 1963: 234, 289; 1960: 79). The third proposition is that the greater the frustration of the threatening group, as might be determined by a history of access-rejections, the greater the likelihood of threatening demands (Lipset, 1960: 74, 79). An initial threat index is the mean of the economic growth rate combined with the mean of the three values of equalitarianism, universalism, and specificity (see Appendix C). This initial threat level is modified as a result of the history of interaction each group develops as it operates in the model. Each time the group works outside the institution and each time access is denied, the demands of the group tend to become larger. For each such experience, two points are subtracted from the threat index. Conversely, for each favorable experience, two points are added to the threat index (see Appendix C). The larger the index number, therefore, the greater likelihood that the threat would be *small*. Once again, a random number is selected to compare with this index number as each group passes through the branch point, and if the number is smaller than the index number, the access demand is granted. And if the number is larger than the index number, the access demand is denied.

The variables we have examined in the preceding four branch points are all related to the question of the stability of the system. The variables we will consider in the remainder of this section are concerned with development toward democratic government. In terms of the operation of the model, this last segment does not come into operation until all five groups have completed five passes through the first part of the model. Thereafter, following each sequence of five passes by the five groups through the first four branch points, one pass is made through the remaining elements of the model.

Branch point 5 enables us to deal with Lipset's concern for the development of a clear distinction between the source of sovereignty and the agents of authority. Figure 3 attempts to detail the variables which will determine whether there will be an increase or a decrease in the identity of the source and agents of authority or whether there will be no change. This formulation makes allowance for the two relevant factors of level of tolerance among all groups and the number of groups that are operating in and outside the established institution (see Appendix C).

The factors which are important for the change in identity of source and agents of authority appear also to be important for the next branch point (no. 6) concerning the conditions for democratic principles. It is assumed that if there is a sufficient level of tolerance among all the groups participating, and a sufficient number of groups are operating within the established institutions, this will provide the necessary condition for possible increase in the acceptance of democratic principles (or rules of the game). Figure 4 illustrates the relationship of group number and tolerance levels. After this initial determination is made in branch point 6, the related branch point (no. 7) concerns a challenge for power by a new political coalition or elite. This branch point involves, again, a random number feature which determines which exit of the branch point is taken. It is assumed here that there is a greater chance of a challenge being made if the effectiveness level is low than if it is high. Hence, if a random number is smaller than the initial effectiveness level, as modified by the mean of

---

If 2 gps are *outside* the institution and total of tol. levels is .LT.180
If 3 gps are *outside* the institution and total of tol. levels is .LT.270
If 4 gps are *outside* the institution and total of tol. levels is .LT.360
If 5 gps are *outside* the institution and total of tol. levels is .LT.450

Then *increase* identity of agents and sources of authority by one point.

If 3 gps are *within* the institution and total of tol. levels is .GT.400
If 4 gps are *within* the institution and total of tol. levels is .GT.325
If 5 gps are *within* the institution and total of tol. levels is .GT.250

Then *reduce* identity of agents and source of authority by one point.

The scale for the degree of identity is initialized at zero. The possibilities that are not covered in the above figure result in no change.

Figure 3: IDENTITY OF AGENTS AND SOURCE OF AUTHORITY FORMULA

If 3 gps are *within* the institution and total tol. levels is .GT.400
If 4 gps are *within* the institution and total tol. levels is .GT.325
If 5 gps are *within* the institution and total tol. levels is .GT.250

Then a greater probability exists for an increase in the acceptance of democratic principles.

Figure 4: ACCEPTANCE OF DEMOCRATIC PRINCIPLES FORMULA

the five tolerance levels (as for branch point 1), then a challenge will not be made. Conversely, if the random number is larger than that level, then a challenge for power will be made. The result will be either an increment or a decrement in the scale of acceptance of democratic principles, starting at the midpoint (50) of the scale. If conditions favoring an increase in acceptance of democratic principles are unfavorable, the challenge will result in a decrease of acceptance by 4 points. If conditions are favorable, the challenge will increase acceptance by 4 points. If no challenge is made under either condition, it will increase acceptance by 2 points under the assumption that continued operation of the system with no challenges for power will to a lesser degree tend toward increased acceptance of the rules of the system (see Appendix C).

Branch point 8 concerns the probability of political conflict leading to a democratic socialization of conflict. This probability level is determined by giving equal weight to acceptance of democratic principles, system tolerance, and the mean of the five group tolerance levels. The mean of these three factors is used as a random number comparison point. If the random number is larger, the democratic socialization of conflict scale (starting at zero) will decrease by one; identification of source and agents of authority will increase by one; and system legitimacy will decrease by five (see Appendix C). If the random number is smaller, the three variables will change in the opposite direction.

After this portion of the flow chart is completed, a new series of group interaction in the first part of the model is initiated. This sequence continues until ten cycles have been completed, the simulation terminated, and the results are calculated and printed. Ten cycles appeared to be sufficient to establish a definite pattern of development for a given set of initial conditions.

A MODEL OF MOORE'S THEORY

OVERVIEW OF THEORY PROPOSITIONS

The theory developed by Moore is designed to explain the historical emergence of democratic government in at least three major nations of the world: Britain, France, and the United States. He also advances propositions relating to the origins of reactionary and communist regimes, but we shall not directly concern ourselves with the patterns he draws for these developments. Our analysis of his book shall be restricted to the examination of the conditions relevant to the development of democratic government.

In contrast to Lipset, Moore posits that a useful sociological explanation of broad social and political changes cannot be undertaken by examining cultural or value patterns. Moore (1966: 486) notes that

> To explain behavior in terms of cultural values is to engage in circular reasoning.... The problem is to determine out of what past and present experiences such an outlook arises and maintains itself. If culture has an empirical meaning, it is as a tendency implanted in the human mind to behave in certain specific ways "acquired by man as a member of society."

To explain social inertia as well as social change, Moore examines what he feels are the crucial experiences which shape the traditions and values of the society. In his historical analysis of the three major nations noted above, although certain values seem to be useful for future development, the decisive factor was not cultural. The crucial factor appeared to be the process by which the transition to commercial agriculture was made. As he states specifically, "the ways in which the landed upper classes and the peasants reacted to the challenge of commercial agriculture were decisive factors in determining political outcome."[16] The eventual outcome of this process would determine which values would become dominant and which would remain from a previous period. New political outcomes, then, emerge from the clash of interests which result when opportunities for social and economic change arise, regardless of whether the current or prevailing value patterns would tend to discourage the pursuit of these new opportunities (Moore, 1966: 421, 422). The transition to commercial agriculture, he admits, is not the only factor involved in determining political outcome. But it is a major one and the one Moore has chosen to focus upon in this explanatory analysis.

Moore warns against attempting to explain social realities through simple quantification techniques. He claims that an adequate description of social life which relies on quantitative measures cannot reflect the qualitative changes in the relations of men or the changes themselves. He then quotes a statement by Whitehead saying that apart from a presupposed pattern, quantity determines nothing (Moore, 1966: 519, 520). In our simulation model, however, there is a presupposed pattern of qualitative relationships which Moore presents in his analysis, and it would appear, therefore, that the quantification necessary for computer simulation would have some relevance to a more specific understanding of the implications of Moore's theory.

The central concern of Moore's analysis is the taming of the agrarian sector in such a way that the political hegemony of the landed upper class is broken or transformed. He notes (1966: 429-430) that

> The peasant had to be turned into a farmer producing for the market instead of for his own consumption and that of the overlord. In this process the landed upper classes either became an important part of the capitalist and democratic tide, as in England, or, if they came to oppose it, they were swept aside in the convulsion of revolution or civil war. In a word, the landed upper classes either helped to make the bourgeois revolution or were destroyed by it.

The theory which Moore develops, then, would apply only to those nations which are in the process of developing a commercial agricultural system out of a previous system of subsistence production. It also implies that there is some commercialization going on in the urban areas of the state providing, thereby, market areas and financial opportunities for the agricultural transformation.

Moore notes that there are three main historical routes from the precommercial world to the modern world. These are through the route of bourgeois revolutions led by commercial classes as in the United States, Britain, and France, the capitalist reactionary revolution from above (which has a weak bourgeois impulse) as in Germany and Japan, and the communist revolution which combines a weak bourgeois impulse with peasant revolt (Moore, 1966: xv, xvi). He goes on to note that India, which is almost unique in its combination of social and colonial conditions, does not fall into any of the three categories. The political outcome in which we are interested for our simulation model is that which results from a strong bourgeois impulse that leads to a liberal and democratic government. This process is seen as

> a long and certainly incomplete struggle to do three closely related things: (1) to check arbitrary rulers, (2) to replace arbitrary rules with just and rational ones, and (3) to obtain a share for the underlying population in the making of rules [Moore, 1966: 414].[17]

The central development in this process is the development of strong and independent commercial interests by an urban bourgeoisie and a strong land-owning commercial class which operates its own rural enterprises. It also implies a reduction in the strength of the traditional landed aristocracy and the elimination of a large class of peasants in the countryside.[18] Other political outcomes result, as noted above, if the landed aristocracy maintains or increases its position of strength or if the peasant population is not reduced in numbers and (apparently) shifted over time to employment in an urban setting. This general framework of development is outlined in the flow chart presented in Appendix B.

As was noted above, the central focus in Moore's conception of economic and political modernization stems from the challenges raised by the move toward a commercialized society in both the urban and rural settings. It is assumed that, in order for rural commercialization to occur, there must first be some commercialization in the urban areas of the country so that there is some profit to be gained by selling rural products for a cash return. This basic starting point is illustrated by branch point 1, which indicates the result of either the absence or the beginning of urban commercial development. As the urban market develops, it will tend to increase the potential for commercializing agriculture and also increase the need for cash by the traditional landed elite. An absence of commercial development will decrease the potential for commercial agricultural production (Moore, 1966: 51, 419, 422).

Branch point 2 indicates an important development within the urban business community, which is necessary if a liberal or democratic system is to emerge. If the business community developing the commercialized economy is able to maintain its independence (in terms of access to capital and making its own economic decisions), it will decrease the probability of a coalition forming between the traditional aristocratic elite and the urban bourgeoisie against the peasants and labor (Moore, 1966: 424, 425, 431). Such a coalition, if it were to form, would tend to develop repressive techniques of rural and urban commercialization rather than allowing independent entrepreneurs the opportunity to operate free from overwhelming governmental interference or control. If the bourgeoisie can develop a strong economic footing, it will tend to develop both interests in opposition to the traditional landed elites and the potential for peaceful competition in political matters.

Although Moore recognizes the importance of violent activity or revolution at some point in most political development processes, this struggle could be minimized if there were other conditions in the cultural heritage of the country which tended to make allowance for the emergence of new interests and recognized a legitimate place for them in the society. Helpful in this process (but not dominant), for example, are values or cultural beliefs in the immunity of certain groups and persons from the power of the ruler, a conception of the right of resistance to unjust authority, and a belief in the importance of contracts made by free agreement among free persons (Moore, 1966: 434-435).

The next point of interest in the developmental process (noted in branch point 3) is whether or not there is a move to commercialize agricultural production. If there is no move to commercialize, then the thrust toward possible democratization of the society is not possible. If commercialization of agriculture does take place, the crucial question is what form this development takes. Of first importance is whether or not a labor-repressive agricultural system is utilized, as noted in branch point 4. If a labor-repressive system is used, it will tend to operate with the aid of the central government, and thereby tend to increase the strength of that central government as well as increasing the potential for a reactionary "revolution from above" as happened in Germany and Japan (Moore, 1966: 434-435). Such a development also tends to reduce the potential for the development of an independent bourgeoisie because of the tendency for the landed elite to maintain its position of commanding strength in political affairs and to use its power to make or direct economic development for its own use (Moore, 1966: 436). This tendency also increases potential for an aristocratic-bourgeois coalition against the peasants.

If labor-repressive agriculture is not used, then the question becomes (as noted by branch point 5) whether or not the commercialization of agriculture results in the elimination of the peasant class. If it is eliminated, this increases the potential for a democratic political system by increasing the potential for development of an independent bourgeoisie and rural commercial class, and by reducing both the strength of the aristocracy, which depends upon peasant agriculture for much of its strength, and the potential for an aristocratic-bourgeois coalition (Moore, 1966: 419-420, 422, 429, 459, 460). If the process of commercialization does not eliminate the peasant class, it will tend to reduce the potential for urban development and increase the potential for peasant revolt as the effects and strains of commercialization are imposed upon the existing structure rather than developing a new social structure which eliminates a class of potential dissidents (Moore, 1966: 395, 406, 430, 473). This will also tend to change the balance of power between the landed aristocracy and the central government by increasing the power of the former and decreasing that of the latter (see Appendix D).

As branch point 6 indicates, if there is an attempt to derive more cash from the peasant without any effort to commercialize, this also increases the potential for peasant revolt. If there is no need for additional cash and no move toward commercialization, there will be no potential change in this variable.

As the new commercial class develops in the urban and rural areas, the development of its independence is enhanced if the older landed aristocracy is enabled to maintain a relatively satisfactory economic position. As noted at branch point 7, if its economic position remains satisfactory, this will increase the potential for the development of independent urban businessmen (Moore, 1966: 425). This assumes that if the traditional elites are too strongly challenged in their economic security, they will be tempted to take repressive political action to curb the influence and potential independence of the commercial classes. This would also seem to imply that a tolerant view of the rising classes by the traditional elite would appear to be more likely if the economy itself were growing rapidly enough to ensure that there were resources to satisfy the traditional elite to prevent it from taking any drastic measures to suppress the independent commercial activities which are challenging it.

As the move toward commercialization proceeds and a period of time lapses, it is assumed by Moore that if the bourgeoisie is gaining strength, the attitudes and values which are important to it will also tend to gain ascendency within the society. This development is illustrated in branch point 8, which indicates that after a period of time, as indicated by the ten passes through the preceding part of the model, there may be a tendency for the society to develop a stronger belief in certain bourgeois values (Moore, 1966: 425). The values affected appear to be those which were cited above as being crucial to the successful development of a liberal bourgeois society, and for the emergence of a democratic government. These values are the belief in immunity of certain groups and persons from the power of the ruler, the conception of the right of resistance to unjust political authority, and the conception of contract by free agreement between free persons.

As the bourgeoisie gains in strength and as its values gain more widespread acceptance, it would seem that there is also a rising potential for what Moore calls the liberal or bourgeois revolution. This would place bourgeois values and the related commercial and industrial activities at the center of the society, and the conflicts and interests emerging from this ascendence would be the primary moving force in the political realm, even though some of the traditional elite may still remain active in political affairs. At least, however, there will be a peaceful competition between the two elites for the support of broader segments of the population through the traditional democratic mechanisms of free speech and election which Moore notes are part of the democratic process (Moore, 1966: 429). Concomitant changes would occur in the potential for the development of an independent urban business class and in central government power, the former increasing and the latter decreasing.

Moore does stress at various points in the book the importance of revolution in shaping the ultimate political outcome of various societies, and he notes (1966: 426-427, 431 and throughout) that even in the transition to democracy there are definite limitations on the possibility of peaceful transition. There are few clear indications given by Moore, however, which specify the significant contributions which such a revolution may bring other than a continued development of those patterns which had been emerging for some time prior to the violent outbreak. The actual prediction of the outcome of specific revolutions is beyond the scope of this model and also, apparently, beyond the scope of the theoretical propositions or generalizations presented by Moore. Too many uncontrolled factors enter in, such as the role of available leadership, the role of external forces, and the various patterns of social relationships which Moore examines primarily in terms of the reactionary revolutions as they occurred in Germany and Japan and the communist peasant revolutions of Russia and China. The examples and propositions derived, therefore, offer little of relevance to the results of a liberal bourgeois revolution. This type of outcome, however, receives some consideration in the model through the accumulation of revolutionary potential and the increase in strength of bourgeois values. The key outcome of the model, then, is not the occurrence of a bourgeois revolution, but an indication of increasing strength by an independent bourgeoisie and the rural commercial class, together with their value system. Concurrently, there should be a tendency for the strength of the landed aristocracy to be reduced and a low potential for an aristocratic-bourgeois coalition. Alternatively, if the potential for a liberal bourgeois revolution is low, then either an increase in the strength of central government and the potential for reactionary revolution will be high, or there will be a high potential for peasant revolt.

BRANCH POINT VARIABLES AND ASSUMPTIONS

As in a previous section, this section will attempt to specify the formulae for determining which exit will be taken at each branch point of the model, and detail the initial conditions and assumptions underlying the sequences of model operation.

This model does not operate in terms of group activity, as does the Lipset model. Rather, it interrelates a sequence of activity which results in increases or decreases in the strength of specified social groups and their values, thereby indicating a potential for democracy. As with the Lipset model, however, we will use 100-point scales to enable us to determine magnitude and direction of movement as the model operates. Several variables will receive an initial ranking on the scales, and they will be modified as a result of model operation. For each simulation run, the two variables used as independent variables (or factors) will be initialized with systematic variation in an attempt to determine their relative impact on the outcome.

There are three primary sets of elements which are relevant for establishing initial conditions. The first relates to the opportunity for commercial and industrial development in urban and rural areas, the second relates to the strength of belief in various values such as corporate and personal immunities, rights of resistance, and freedom of contract, and the third comprises the power levels of the two crucial predevelopment political groups—the central government and the landed aristocracy. With regard to the first set, it is assumed that the opportunity for urban development will be sufficient for an initial move in that direction, since Moore's generalizations hinge on the fact that the development he describes (1966: 422) is a result of the impact of urban commercialization and the potential it opens for agricultural commercialization. The level of opportunity for agricultural development will be initialized at the midpoint on the scale in each simulation run. In terms of the theory, it can never be at an initial level higher than that for urban commercialization.

Each of the cultural values will be initialized on a 100-point scale and varied with each simulation run. The assumption is made that the initial strength of these values will equally become higher as the power of the central government and that of the landed aristocracy approaches a balance (Moore, 1966: 415, 416). The third set of elements has one essential variation. This is the relative strength of the central government as opposed to the strength of the landed aristocracy. It is assumed that they are inversely related and that if they approach a balance, as noted above, they will approach the medieval feudal ideal of the Western European system (Moore, 1966: 422, 459). Because they are inversely related, the power level of one—the central government—will be varied systematically as an initial condition and as one of two independent variables. Five levels will be used (90, 75, 50, 25, 10) to represent the 100-point scale range of high to low levels. This variation will control the initial levels of aristocratic power (as noted above) and also the initial levels of the three cultural levels. The initial level of the values varies positively with the balance between central government and aristocratic power. Consequently only three value levels are needed to correspond with the five power levels listed above (100 for the 50 level, 50 for the 75 and 25 levels, and 20 for the 90 and 10 levels) based on the formula $A = 100 - |X-Y|$ where A = value levels, X = central government, and Y = aristocracy power levels.

The other independent variable for this model is the rate of growth of per capita GNP, also initialized on a 100-point scale. As with the Lipset model, 90 = high, 50 = medium, and 10 = low rates of growth.

With these considerations about initial conditions and independent variables in mind, we may turn to the first branch point (see Appendix B) which determines whether or not commercial development is occurring in urban areas. As an initial condition, we may use an arbitrary level of 75 on the 100-point scale on the assumption that the model as a whole is relevant only if there is some initial impetus for commercialization of the urban areas. Subsequent operation of the model can modify this initial potential in either direction. As with the Lipset model, a random number is chosen and compared to this initial potential level of commercialization. If it is more than that level, it will decrease by one point the potential for commercializing agriculture. If it is less than or equal to that level, the opposite exit is taken, resulting in an increase in that potential on the assumption that urban markets will be developed and a start made on the transportation necessary for transporting goods for the urban market. The development of urban commercial interests will also increase by one point the need for cash by the landed elite, who will be tempted to purchase items made available to it by growing urban commercial market activity. It is further assumed that, once an initial need for cash by the landed elite has been established (initialized at 10), it will tend to remain, even though urban commercialization may stagnate.

At branch point 2, the potential for development of an independent business class will tend to be higher if the complex of the three bourgeois values are higher. As noted above, it is assumed that these three values will become stronger as a balance is approached between the strength of the landed elite and that of the central government. It is also assumed that the three values of immunity, right of resistance, and freedom of contract are all equally important and shall, therefore, receive an equally proportionate weight in determining the initial index number of this branch point. The mean of the three values (up to a maximum of 90) shall be used as the initial potential for development of an independent business class. As the model operates, this initial level will change to indicate varying levels of potential. If the yes exit is taken, it will increase by one the independent power of the bourgeoisie, and, as noted before, this will also tend to decrease by one the potential of an aristocratic-bourgeois coalition under the assumption that a growing and strong bourgeois element will be better able to assert its independence from other sources of social and economic strength. If the no exit is taken, there will be a decrease in strength of the bourgeoisie and an increased potential of an aristocratic-bourgeois coalition formed against the peasant and worker classes (see Appendix D). The bourgeois power level starts from zero.

The preceding elements of the model help to structure the potential for development of commercial agriculture as indicated in branch point 3. The initial level of opportunity for development of commercial agriculture will be set at 50 to give an even chance for commercial development because the model is designed to illustrate a potential social and political impact of rural commercialization. Nevertheless, the continued operation of the model will affect the potential for development of commercial agriculture, and therefore affect the direction of change for the system. If the random number is lower than or equal to the potential level, the model immediately goes on to determine the type of commercial agriculture that is developed. If the random number is higher, a determination is then made concerning the potential for change in extracting more surplus from the peasants, even though actual commercialization is not attempted.

Branch point 4 raises the first of two questions on the type of agricultural commercialization that is developed. At this point, the question is whether or not labor-repressive agriculture is used, a system which utilizes the power and authority of the central government to extract more surplus from the peasant class. It is assumed that the potential for using labor-repressive agriculture will be higher if the strength of the central government is higher (Moore, 1966: 422, 434, 435). It is also assumed that this potential will be modified downward if the values of corporate and personal immunities and right of resistance are higher. The random number comparison point of this potential is determined by the formula: Potential = $(100-A+2B)/3$, where A = the mean of the values and B = central government power level. If the random number is smaller than or equal to this potential central government power, the potential for reactionary revolution, and the potential for aristocratic-bourgeois coalition are increased by one, while the potential for development of an independent bourgeoisie is reduced by one (see Appendix D). If the random number is higher, another relevant question is posed at the next branch point.

Branch point 5 determines whether the commercial development of agriculture removes the peasants as a class and replaces them with a class of independent small landowners who have entered the commercial market system. It is assumed that the potential for elimination of the peasant class will be higher if the value of free contract among free persons is higher in that society and strength of aristocracy is low. The formula for determining the potential is $(100-A+B)/2$, where A = strength of aristocracy and B = level of the free contract value (see Appendix D). If the random number is lower than or equal to this number, the yes exit is taken, and the potential for urban commercialization will be increased by one on the assumption that it will increase the availability of cash for capital investment. It will also improve the independent position of the bourgeoisie (by one point) because of the increased availability of capital not under the direct control of either the state or the landed aristocracy. And, of course, it will increase by one point the strength of the rural commercial class and reduce by the same amount both the strength of the landed aristocracy and the potential for an aristocratic-bourgeois coalition. If the number is higher and the no exit is taken, it will reduce by one the potential for urban development (Moore, 1966: 395, 406, 430). This development would also increase the potential for peasant revolt by one point and change the balance of power between the landed aristocracy and the central government by increasing the former by one point and decreasing the latter by the same amount (see Appendix D).

This leads to consideration of branch point 6, which also has an option for increasing the potential for peasant revolt based on the level of need for cash by the landed elite, even though they are not attempting to commercialize agriculture. The initial level of this need shall be set at an arbitrary low figure of ten. This level will be affected by the development of urban commercialization as noted above in connection with branch point 1. An increased need for cash by the landed elite will increase the potential for peasant revolt by one point, whereas an absence of such a need brings no change.

As the system and the strength of the commercial classes develop, they will have an effect on the economic position of the landed aristocracy. At branch point 7, it is assumed that the economic position of the landed aristocracy will remain sufficient if the strength of the immunities and free contract values are high, and if there is a rapid development of the economy as defined by rate of GNP growth. The index for branch point 7 will be the mean of the three factors mentioned; the rate of economic growth (weighted to be 3 times more important than the values) and the immunities and freedom of contract value levels. If the random number is smaller than or equal to this number, the yes exit is taken and the potential for development of independent businessmen is increased by 3 points. If the number is larger, the no exit is taken and the contrary adjustment made (see Appendix D).

After ten passes through the above flow chart, indicating a passage of time, branch point 8 will determine whether the ascendency of the commercial classes is sufficient. The potential level will be determined by summing the strengths of the rural commercial interests and the strengths of the bourgeoisie, both of which have started from a zero level of a 100-point scale. Again a random number is chosen to compare to this level and if the number is equal to or smaller than the sum, the yes exit is taken and it would indicate that the commercial classes had gained sufficient strength to have an effect on the general acceptance of these values. Each of the three values is increased, therefore, by 10 points. The potential for urban development by independent businessmen increases by 5 points, the power of the central government is reduced by 5, and the potential for a bourgeois revolution is increased by 1 point (see Appendix D). If the number is larger and the no exit is taken, no change is recorded. After this determination is made, the simulation returns to the first part of the flow chart and continues the entire sequence for a total of ten cycles.

ANALYSIS OF MOORE MODEL DATA

The data generated by the Moore model[19] were the result of fifty simulation runs for each of fifteen patterns combining different levels of two factors (or independent variables) as measured by five dependent variables (or measures). Factor A (rate of per capita GNP growth) was tested on three levels, and factor B (central government power) was tested on five levels. The purpose of the analysis was to determine the effect, if any, of the two factors upon the dependent measures. Tests were needed that could indicate significance of effect and also enable one to gain greater insight into the pattern of relationships which could assist in detailing more precisely the implications of the modeled theory.

Main Effects

The initial statistical test most appropriate for these purposes appeared to be a 3x5 analysis of variance (ANOVA) testing the null hypothesis of no treatment effects. If this test indicated significance by rejection of the null hypothesis for several measures, other tests could indicate more precisely the pattern of effects.

Univariate ANOVA could not be relied upon exclusively, however, because the dependent measures were not entirely independent measures of effects, as indicated in Table 1. Of ten possible relationships, five indicate negative or positive correlations above the 0.5 level. The pattern of correlations displayed tends to confirm predicted results and gives some confidence that the model generates outputs which correspond to general theory patterns and requirements. Correlation between bourgeois power, rural commercialization, and bourgeois revolution, for example, indicate that bourgeois power can develop without extensive rural commercialization, but that, if this line of development is followed, there is less chance of bourgeois revolution or democratic development occurring. The latter point is indicated by the higher correlation between bourgeois revolution and rural commercialization (0.605) than between bourgeois revolution and bourgeois power (0.534). These correlations were expected, but, because of the dependency problem involved, it was useful to perform a multivariate ANOVA (MANOVA) to give an indication of the reliability of the univariate ANOVA. If only a few or no linear combinations of the MANOVA were significant, then little or no importance could be attached to an indication of univariate ANOVA significance of main or interaction effects.

With these factors and caveats in mind, we may turn to an analysis of the simulation data. In general, the statistical analysis revealed that the greatest overall impact on the dependent measures was a result of B effects, the relative power of the central government. Changes in this factor had a more uniform effect on all the measures than did factor A, the rate of economic growth, and this relationship is demonstrated by several displays of statistical analysis results examined below.

The MANOVA analysis for factor B as compared to factor A (Table 2) indicates the stronger effect of the former.[20] All four linear combinations (or roots) of factor B are significant at the .001 level of confidence, whereas only one of two combinations achieves this level for factor A. Where all linear combinations are significant, one can interpret the univariate ANOVA and other tests with confidence. Where one of two combinations is significant, more caution is required, but some conclusions may be at least tentatively drawn.

Two tests based upon the MANOVA (Standardized Discriminant Function Coefficients, and Correlations Between Dependent Variables and Maximum Variance Linear Combinations) and the univariate ANOVA F tests give insight into which variable or measures were most affected by factor variation. The F tests of Table 3, interpreted in the light of

TABLE 1
CORRELATIONS BETWEEN DEPENDENT MEASURES[a]

Variable	Bour Power	Rural Com.	Peasant Rev.	Coalition	Bour Rev.
Bour power	—				
Rural com.	0.298	—			
Peasant rev.	0.031	-0.282	—		
Coalition	-0.914	-0.581	-0.083	—	
Bour rev.	0.534	0.605	-0.075	-0.661	—

a. Values exceeding .273 are significant at the .05 level of confidence. See Appendix B for listing of terms used in tables.

TABLE 2
MANOVA TESTS OF SIGNIFICANCE USING WILKS LAMBDA CRITERION

	Root	F	DFHYP	DFERR	P Less Than
Factor A	1	277.901	10.000	1462.000	0.001
(GNP)	2	0.561	4.000	731.500	0.691
Factor B	1	553.211	20.000	2425.403	0.001
(central	2	303.542	12.000	2019.870	0.001
gov.)	3	18.771	6.000	1464.000	0.001
	4	11.776	2.000	732.500	0.001

TABLE 3
UNIVARIATE ANOVA F TESTS

	Factor A (GNP) d.f. 2,735 P Less Than[a]	Factor B (central gov.) d.f. 4,735 P Less Than[a]
Bour power	0.01	0.01
Rural com.	0.01	0.01
Peasant rev.	0.71	0.01
Coalition	0.01	0.01
Bour rev.	0.01	0.01

a. Results were significant at the .001 level of confidence, but are listed at .01 level because of dependency.

MANOVA significance, display the broad B effect on all measures. The relative power position of the central government had a significant effect on all variables. The display for factor A indicates at least some significant A effects on all variables except the potential for peasant revolt. The rate of economic growth appears to have little relevance to this potential, a finding reinforced by the Scheffé test results discussed below.

The MANOVA-related tests (Table 4) again indicate the dependency problem for factor A. Only one linear combination was significant. The correlations of variables to that combination, however, indicate that A effects were greater upon bourgeois power and the potential for an aristocratic-bourgeois coalition, the first positively and the second negatively correlated. This is a finding not inconsistent with the verbal theory, tending to confirm the importance of economic growth for development of an independent business class.

Tests for B effects indicate that four linear combinations were significant, demonstrating a broad effect on the dependent measures. The most significant linear combination for this factor is highly correlated with rural commercialization (positively) and aristocratic-bourgeois coalition

TABLE 4
MANOVA-RELATED TESTS

	Standardized Discriminant Function Coefficients[a]				Correlations Between Dependent Variables and Maximum Variance Linear Combinations			
	1	2	3	4	1	2	3	4
Factor A								
Bour power	1.067				0.955			
Rural com.	-0.147				0.084			
Peasant rev.	-0.092				0.010			
Coalition	-0.087				-0.790			
Bour rev.	-0.271				0.274			
Factor B								
Bour power	-1.227	1.403	-1.073	-1.923	0.445	0.371	-0.757	0.299
Rural com.	0.197	0.797	0.050	-1.386	0.650	0.532	0.341	0.184
Peasant rev.	0.188	-0.580	-0.339	-0.554	0.311	-0.852	-0.310	-0.120
Coalition	-2.085	1.255	-1.292	-2.238	-0.724	-0.312	0.472	-0.383
Bour rev.	-0.559	-0.196	0.057	1.139	0.271	0.248	-0.085	0.797

a. These are the linear combinations tested by the MANOVA by column in order of significance. Less than two columns indicates the failure of the second linear combination of the treatments to be significant. The values listed are the coefficients of the linear combination being tested. Hence if Y_1 and Y_2 are tested in the MANOVA (using Factor B as an example), then $Y_1 = -1.227 \times$ (Bour Power) $+ 0.197 \times$ (Rural Com.) $\times \sigma$ Rural Com. ... $-0.559 \times$ (Bour Rev.) $\times \sigma$ Bour Rev. $Y_2 = 1.403 \times$ (Bour Power) ... $-0.196 \times$ (Bour Rev.) $\times \sigma$ Bour Rev.

The correlations are those between the dependent measures and Y_1 or Y_2, i.e., Y_1, Y_2 are treated as new variables which are independent.

potential (negatively). This pattern is maintained in the second combination, where the expected negative correlation with peasant revolt potential appears. These correlations should not be burdened, however, with too much dependence for establishing firm relationships between factor and measure. They are useful primarily for illustrating patterns which other statistical displays and tests can confirm or deny with more confidence and reliability. An examination of the marginal means along with the Scheffé test of individual mean differences, discussed below, will bear the bulk of this burden, although it should be noted that the Scheffé test examines univariate linear contrasts for significance and therefore contains the same weaknesses as the univariate F tests.

Interaction

Table 5 indicates that only two of five linear combinations were significantly affected by AB interaction. This demonstrates that, although interaction effects were present, they were very weak, even though the univariate F tests show interaction effects for four of five variables (Table 6).[21] The weakness of AB effects was demonstrated further when graphic displays of AB interactions indicated that for three measures there was a very uniform direction of impact with only the slightest indication of interaction effects. For two variables closely associated with democratic development, bourgeois power, and bourgeois revolution potential, the graphic display indicated a slight interaction effect. The most apparent theoretical explanation for this is that at the highest level of economic growth there is a favorable climate for the development of conditions conducive to democratic politics above what would normally be expected given the more adverse balance of power (B_3 is optimal) between the central government and the landed aristocracy. This is a finding not clarified by the original verbal theory. The interaction also appears to indicate that, at an optimal B level, an intermediate economic growth rate can produce results favorable for democratic development usually attained only at higher rates of growth.

Mean and Mean Differences

Because the MANOVA and ANOVA tests indicated significant A and B effects, there was justification for using the Scheffé post-hoc test of individual mean differences.[22] This test together with an evaluation of marginal means gives some insight into model results useful for theory elaboration.

TABLE 5
MANOVA TEST OF SIGNIFICANCE USING WILKS LAMBDA CRITERION FOR AB INTERACTION

Root	F	DFHYP	DFERR	P Less Than
1	25.773	40.000	3189.150	0.001
2	8.721	28.000	3080.969	0.001
3	1.237	18.000	2932.000	0.221
4	0.619	10.000	2724.546	0.799
5	0.181	4.000	2433.403	0.948

TABLE 6
UNIVARIATE ANOVA F TESTS OF AB INTERACTION EFFECTS

Variable	P Less Than[a]	d.f. 8,735
Bour power	0.01	—
Rural com.	0.01	—
Peasant rev.	0.139	—
Coalition	0.01	—
Bour rev.	0.01	—

a. The 0.01 results were significant at the 0.001 level of confidence, but are listed at 0.01 level because of dependency.

Examination of Tables 7 and 8 reveals that there were significant differences between the levels (or treatments) of factor A in their effect upon three of five measures—bourgeois power, aristocratic-bourgeois coalition potential, and bourgeois revolution potential. This pattern reflects the importance, in a very specific way, of the rate of economic growth for the development of an independent business class which is not repressed or induced to form a restrictive coalition with the landed aristocracy. The result was a higher potential for a successful bourgeois revolution and the establishment of conditions for a democratic polity. This last potential, however, appears to be limited to the highest level of development, since only the A_1 treatment produced a positive level of bourgeois power and a negative coalition potential. The lower levels of economic growth were not sufficient and were not significantly different, as the A_2 and A_3 contrast for bourgeois revolution indicates.

The theory posits factor B as having the major effect upon rural commercialization and potential for peasant revolt, and this is confirmed by both the post-hoc test and the marginal mean pattern. It was not anticipated, however, that there would be no significant contrasts for factor A in reference to these two measures.[23] This is an important

TABLE 7
MARGINAL MEANS

Factor Level	Bour Power	Rural Com.	Peasant Rev.	Coalition	Bour Rev.
A_1	61.680	20.640	37.544	- 46.936	3.688
A_2	-16.786	18.756	37.472	35.884	2.120
A_3	-57.904	17.448	37.136	80.368	1.376
B_1	-51.200	2.207	20.093	122.067	0.640
B_2	-10.120	11.507	23.140	59.700	2.050
B_3	72.986	53.860	22.960	-107.480	5.880
B_4	5.360	21.887	52.180	- 7.920	2.387
B_5	-38.706	5.280	68.547	49.160	1.027

NOTE: A sixth variable was used to measure potential for reactionary revolution. Analysis revealed, however, that this measure was functionally related to three other measures such that Bour Power + Rural Com. + Coalition = Reac. Rev., a plausible, but unexpected result. The Reac. Rev. measure could not, therefore, be incorporated in the statistical analysis, but the sums of the marginal means are listed below as a convenient reference.

	Reac. Rev.		Reac. Rev.
A_1	35.384	B_1	73.074
A_2	37.854	B_2	61.087
A_3	39.912	B_3	19.366
		B_4	19.327
		B_5	15.734

finding, indicating that the relative strength of the central government is the dominating or controlling factor for these two variables.

Superficial examination of analysis data in Tables 7 and 8 for factor B does not reveal a meaningful pattern. A pattern does emerge, however, if two special features of this factor are recalled. First, that central government power is negatively correlated with the power of the landed aristocracy. Second, when the two reach a balance (at the B_3 level), there is theoretically the optimal propensity for bourgeois revolution. Consequently (as is most clearly displayed in Table 7), the B_3 level is the peak of a somewhat normal curve for the variables most closely associated with bourgeois revolution (Bour. Power and Rural Com. positively and Coalition negatively), as well as for the bourgeois revolution measure itself. This corresponds with theory propositions. It also helps explain the absence of significant contrasts at several points in the table for these measures. The nonsignificant contrasts occur in each case where comparisons were made between factor levels occupying similar but opposite "tail" positions of the normal curve pattern centered on B_3. In three cases,

TABLE 8
SCHEFFE TEST ON A[a]

$$F = \frac{\bar{X} - \bar{X}}{S_w^2 (n_1 + n_2) / n_1 n_2}$$

$F' = (J-1) F_{(.01)}$

$F' = 2(4.62) = 9.240$

F scores (significant scores in boldface)

	Bour Power	Rural Com.	Peasant Rev.	Coalition	Bour Rev.
$A_1 \& A_2$	**413.187**	2.682	0.003	**278.453**	**36.147**
$A_1 \& A_3$	**959.689**	7.700	0.124	**657.910**	**78.602**
$A_2 \& A_3$	**113.461**	1.292	0.084	**80.332**	8.132

SCHEFFE TEST ON B[a]

$F' = 4(3.34) = 13.360$

$B_1 \& B_2$	**113.251**	**65.374**	6.964	**157.903**	**28.823**
$B_1 \& B_3$	**1034.974**	**2016.653**	6.165	**2139.074**	**403.779**
$B_1 \& B_4$	**214.685**	**292.745**	**772.374**	**685.934**	**44.882**
$B_1 \& B_5$	10.475	7.137	**1761.282**	**215.784**	2.191
$B_2 \& B_3$	**463.499**	**1355.839**	0.024	**1134.622**	**216.838**
$B_2 \& B_4$	**16.081**	**81.439**	**632.648**	**185.623**	1.764
$B_2 \& B_5$	**54.839**	**29.308**	**1546.732**	4.509	**15.088**
$B_3 \& B_4$	**306.910**	**772.692**	**640.516**	**402.394**	**179.426**
$B_3 \& B_5$	**837.198**	**1783.836**	**1559.020**	**996.065**	**346.338**
$B_4 \& B_5$	**130.314**	**208.459**	**200.958**	**132.266**	**27.191**

a. This post-hoc comparison indicates a significant difference if the F score equals or exceeds the F' score. The formulae, descriptions, and F table information were drawn from Ferguson (1966: 296, 297, 411).

the comparison was between B_1 and B_5, and one case each comparing B_2 and B_5 and B_2 and B_4. This pattern is compatible with theory propositions and demonstrates the importance of the B_3 level for bourgeois revolution potential and the emergence of a democratic polity.

Despite the approximation of a normal curve, the other B levels are not equally important for the variables contributing toward democratic development, a finding not clarified by the theory. Table 8 data indicate that, comparing B_2 and B_4 and B_1 and B_5, the lower levels of government power (B_4 and B_5) offer greater potential for such development than higher levels (B_1 and B_2). This is true for all four relevant variables, although it must be noted that the B_2 and B_4 contrast is not significant for bourgeois revolution potential. The contrasts are significant for the other three measures, however, tending to confirm this general proposition.[24]

The importance of the B3 level for democratic development is also illustrated (Table 8) by the effects upon peasant and reactionary revolution potential, the former increasing sharply when central government power is low and the latter increasing in the converse situation. The former trend is also confirmed by the F score pattern which is shaped by this sharp difference in effect.

A comparison of the two effect patterns also gives tentative support to the previous general conclusion concerning the relatively greater importance of lower levels of factor B for democratic development. The potential for reactionary revolution increases more sharply than does the potential for peasant revolution as B moves from the B_3 level. Assuming no necessary mutual exclusiveness of developing potentials, the latter appears to be more compatible with democratic development.

ANALYSIS OF LIPSET MODEL DATA

The data generated by the Lipset model were the result of 50 simulation runs of 27 patterns combining different levels of three factors (or independent variables) as measured by six dependent variables (or measures). Factor A (rate of per capita GNP growth), factor B (economic values pattern), and factor C (political values pattern) were each tested on three levels. The analysis was designed to indicate the effect, if any, of the three factors upon the dependent measures using, among other things, tests of significance that would give insight into several possible interaction effects, as well as main effects.

Main Effects

As with the Moore model, the dependent measures were not independent as indicated by the correlations of Table 9. Of fifteen possible relationships, twelve indicate negative or positive correlations above the 0.5 level. The pattern of correlations displayed was expected for the most part. The high correlations with legitimacy (negative and positive) in column one, the negative correlations with identification of source and agents of authority, and the positive correlations between acceptance of democratic principles, number of groups within, and group tolerance correspond in general to the broad outline of theory expectations, giving an additional basis for confidence in the validity of the model as an accurate representation of the theory. A higher positive correlation was expected, however, between democratic socialization of conflict and the last-named three variables. This could be an indication of a weakness in the model, or it could point toward the difficulty of achieving this democratic goal. The high correlation with legitimacy and identification (positive and negative, respectively) is an indication that the latter conclusion is more accurate, since these correlations do agree with the pattern of expected results. If all five correlations with socialization had been unexpected, the former conclusion would have been the one more obviously correct, and additional sensitivity testing would have been in order.

In any case, high correlations between dependent measures do exist. To attach any importance to a 3x3x3 univariate analysis of variance (ANOVA) significance test of treatment effects, therefore, a multivariate analysis of variance (MANOVA) would also have to indicate significance for the effects tested.

The MANOVA analysis (Table 10) indicates that factors A and B had a stronger effect on the dependent measures than did factor C.[25] Two of two linear combinations (or roots) are significant at the .001 level of confidence for factors A and B, whereas only one of two combinations achieves this level for factor C. These results demonstrate the need for caution in interpreting C effects in univariate ANOVA.

The univariate ANOVA F tests (Table 11) indicate significance of effects for all factors on all measures. Rate of per capita GNP growth, economic values, and political values appear to have had an equally broad impact upon these variables. This means that both political stability and democratic potential were affected independently by the levels of these independent variables indicating that, apart from the modifications produced by interaction effects noted below, higher levels of these factors will each contribute to greater stability and democracy. The significance of the C effects, however, must be qualified because of the failure of the

TABLE 9
CORRELATIONS BETWEEN DEPENDENT VARIABLES[a]

	Legit.	Ident.	Accept.	Social	No. Groups	Tolerance
Legit.	—					
Ident.	-0.832	—				
Accept.	0.675	-0.702	—			
Social	0.608	-0.805	0.322	—		
No. groups	0.544	-0.560	0.549	0.265	—	
Tolerance	0.835	-0.702	0.738	0.327	0.608	—

a. Values exceeding .273 are significant at the .05 level of confidence. See Appendix A for listing of terms used in tables.

second-best linear combination to be significant. But post-hoc analysis based on these indications of significance appear to be justified, thereby permitting a greater discrimination to be made relating factor effect to individual measure.

Before proceeding to post-hoc analysis, the MANOVA-related tests can give some preliminary insights into univariate effects. Table 12 again indicates the dependency problem for factor C. Only one linear combination was significant. The correlations of dependent variables with the maximum variance linear combination that was tested, however, indicate that the single linear combination that was significant depended more highly upon tolerance and democratic socialization of conflict (social) than upon the other measures. This relationship of factor C to socialization was expected in terms of the theory, but conclusions about its importance relative to factors A and B must be qualified in light of the post-hoc test examined below. The relationship of tolerance to factor C displayed in Table 12 was not expected, although it is not inconsistent with the theory.

TABLE 10
MANOVA TESTS OF SIGNIFICANCE USING
WILKS LAMBDA CRITERION

Factor	Root	F	DFHYP	DFERR	P Less Than
A (GNP)	1	290.660	12.000	2636.000	0.001
	2	28.512	5.000	1318.500	0.001
B (econ. values)	1	973.475	12.000	2636.000	0.001
	2	174.133	5.000	1318.500	0.001
C (pol. values)	1	106.658	12.000	2636.000	0.001
	2	0.751	5.000	1318.000	0.586

TABLE 11
UNIVARIATE ANOVA F TESTS

d.f. = 2,1323

Variable	Factor A (GNP) P Less Than[a]	Factor B (econ. values) P Less Than[a]	Factor C (pol. values) P Less Than[a]
Legit.	0.01	0.01	0.01
Ident.	0.01	0.01	0.01
Accept.	0.01	0.01	0.01
Social	0.01	0.01	0.01
No. groups	0.01	0.01	0.01
Tolerance	0.01	0.01	0.01

a. Results were significant at the .001 level of confidence, but are listed at .01 because of dependency.

TABLE 12
MANOVA-RELATED TESTS

	Variable	Standardized Discriminant Function Coefficients[a] 1	2	Correlations Between Dependent Variables and Maximum Variance Linear Combinations 1	2
A (GNP)	Legit.	2.109	0.879	0.670	0.064
	Ident.	0.904	0.179	-0.264	0.148
	Accept.	-0.026	0.121	0.242	-0.127
	Social	-0.183	-0.122	0.170	-0.017
	No. groups	0.469	-1.176	0.455	-0.788
	Tolerance	-0.974	-0.041	0.359	-0.098
B (econ. values)	Legit.	2.130	-0.902	0.717	0.110
	Ident.	0.598	-0.887	-0.328	-0.365
	Accept.	-0.063	-0.307	0.281	0.251
	Social	-0.332	-0.224	0.220	0.138
	No. groups	0.383	1.023	0.444	0.845
	Tolerance	-1.053	0.073	0.385	0.265
C (pol. values)	Legit.	-0.865		0.525	
	Ident.	0.635		-0.524	
	Accept.	-0.323		0.279	
	Social	1.121		0.538	
	No. groups	-0.185		0.240	
	Tolerance	1.861		0.708	

a. These are the linear combinations tested by the MANOVA by column in order of significance. Less than two columns indicates the failure of the second linear combination of the treatments to be significant. (See Table 4 for further discussion of these MANOVA tests.)

The MANOVA-related tests for A and B effects indicate that the greatest impact for both was upon legitimacy, and secondarily upon the number of groups operating within the system. The legitimacy measure displays a .670 correlation with the most significant linear combination for factor A, and a .717 correlation for factor B. The second highest correlation in both cases is the number of groups within, correlated .455 with factor A combination and .444 with factor B. These correlation patterns were predicted in terms of the theory. The additional expectation that the greatest impact would be upon legitimacy is also tentatively confirmed. The more tentative expectation that B effects would be more important for the number of groups within, however, is not confirmed by this test, and this finding is reinforced by the post-hoc test discussed below. The examination of marginal means and mean differences will give greater insight into specific relationships and provide firmer confirmation of findings.

Interactions

The data displayed in Tables 13 and 14 indicate that several interaction effects were significant. This is especially true of the AB and BC interactions, both of which obtained significance for three of four MANOVA linear combinations as compared to two of four for AC interaction.

Graphing of the AB interactions indicated that effects were uniform over the six dependent measures. For all six measures, A_2 exceeded A_1 at intersection B_2, and A_3 neared the A_1 level. This is a strong indication of the disruptive effect of rapid economic growth if economic values are too traditional and ascriptive. More moderate rates of economic growth tend to produce near equal or better results for both stability and democracy if there is a mixed commitment to modernizing economic values. This both confirms expectations and gives greater specificity to the theory.

The table and graph data for AC interaction effects indicate that they are very moderate. Effects are significant for those measures which are primarily related to political stability. Graphic analysis reveals that the greatest interaction impact is upon the number of groups operating within the political institutional framework. For all levels of factor C (commitment to modern political values), A_2 exceeds A_1. This pattern was

TABLE 13
MANOVA TESTS OF SIGNIFICANCE FOR INTERACTION USING WILKS LAMBDA CRITERION

	Root	F	DFHYP	DFERR	P Less Than
AB	1	174.110	24.000	4599.163	0.001
	2	8.634	15.000	3729.852	0.001
	3	3.118	8.000	2638.000	0.002
	4	0.461	3.000	1319.500	0.709
AC	1	10.190	24.000	4599.163	0.001
	2	3.073	15.000	3729.852	0.001
	3	0.939	8.000	2638.000	0.483
	4	0.805	3.000	1319.500	0.491
BC	1	39.715	24.000	4599.163	0.001
	2	6.607	15.000	3729.852	0.001
	3	3.238	8.000	2638.000	0.001
	4	1.193	3.000	1319.500	0.311
ABC	1	6.022	48.000	6489.175	0.001
	2	2.762	35.000	6188.920	0.001
	3	2.216	24.000	5796.504	0.001
	4	0.985	15.000	5281.500	0.468
	5	0.845	8.000	4607.163	0.563
	6	0.719	3.000	3735.852	0.540

TABLE 14
UNIVARIATE ANOVA F TESTS FOR INTERACTION

	P Less Than[a]			
	AB d.f. 4,1323	AC d.f. 4,1323	BC d.f. 4,1323	ABC d.f. 8,1323
Legit.	0.01	0.01	0.01	0.01
Ident.	0.01	0.288	0.01	0.133
Accept.	0.01	0.024	0.01	0.253
Social	0.01	0.833	0.01	0.541
No. groups	0.01	0.01	0.01	0.01
Tolerance	0.01	0.01	0.01	0.01

a. The 0.01 results were significant at the 0.001 level of confidence, but are listed at 0.01 level because of dependency.

unexpected, and the reason for it is not clear. There is no apparent reason, in terms of the theory or otherwise, why moderate economic growth induces more groups to operate within the political institutions than higher growth rates, given any of the three levels of commitment to modern political values. It indicates that rapid economic growth has a destabilizing effect regardless of the political value pattern. It should be remembered, however, that the AC interaction graph has averaged B effects, and given the interaction between A and B it might explain why, on the average, in relation to factor C, moderate economic growth is a more stabilizing factor. This interpretation conforms to theory propositions and indicates the powerful effect of the AB interaction.

Significant BC interactions were obtained on all six measures. The pattern which emerges is again related to the question of congruence between factors, this time between economic and political values. The propensities for stability and democracy are enhanced if commitment to modern values is approximately at the same level in both the economic and the political subsystems. Again, this is an expected pattern, and the demonstration that effects were significant for all measures produced additional insight into theory implications.

Significant ABC interactions were obtained on three of six linear combinations (Table 13) and on three of six measures (Table 14). The dependency of measures again requires that conclusions be tentative. Graphic analysis of ABC interactions revealed a pattern of effects which is best exemplified by the tolerance measure. For this measure, there appear to be interaction effects resulting from a congruence of level for all three factors. In general, higher levels of tolerance were obtained when economic growth and economic and political value commitment were at similar levels on the high, medium, and low scales. This pattern was obtained to some degree—for the other five measures (with Ident. displaying the expected inverse relationship), and it supplements the findings noted above concerning the importance of factor-level congruence for two factor interaction effects.

Marginal Means and Mean Differences

The indications of significant A, B, and C effects noted previously warrant the use of the Scheffé post-hoc test for individual mean differences. An examination of both the marginal means (Table 15) and the post-hoc tests (Table 16) makes apparent the generally broader impact of factor B on the dependent measures. The highest and lowest mean values on all measures (except Ident.) and the greatest number of significant mean differences (16 of 18) are associated with factor B. Using the same criteria, factor A appears to be next in general impact and factor C the weakest. This conforms to the findings on C effects noted above. There were no theoretical propositions or expectations regarding this hierarchy of impact. This finding represents, therefore, an elaboration of theory implications. Given the previously noted relationships between economic values (factor B) and economic growth (factor A) in regard to their impact upon democratic development, it might be stated as a general proposition that, of the factors considered, the degree of acceptance of modern economic values is the dominant factor in determining whether or not moderate to rapid economic growth will lead to a payoff of stable democratic government, given at least a moderate acceptance of modern political values. In other words, if one of the three factors is low compared to the other two, it is best for democratic stability if the low factor is not factor B.

Examining factors individually, we note that there is but one significant difference between A_1 and A_2 among the six measures. This indicates the very similar impact on outcome of high and moderate levels of economic growth.[26] This might best be explained by recalling the AB interaction that was prominent in the preceding section. Since the marginal means average the other two factors, the lack of significance between A_1 and A_2 indicates that, on the average for all levels of B and C, a moderate level of economic growth produces outcomes similar to high levels of growth because of the detrimental effects of discrepancies between growth rate and value patterns, especially economic values. This again clarifies for the theory the importance of moderate rates of economic growth for the "average" case of political development, which might be presumed not to have a high acceptance of modern economic values.

TABLE 15
MARGINAL MEANS[a]–LIPSET MODEL

Factor Level	Legit.	Ident.	Accept.	Social	No. Groups	Tolerance
A_1	20.084	2.075	40.888	-1.977	2.624	25.382
A_2	21.275	1.302	42.737	-1.875	3.222	28.117
A_3	- 91.866	7.313	27.591	-4.040	1.288	- 6.775
B_1	116.413	3.353	53.422	0.186	3.706	52.255
B_2	4.924	0.473	43.302	-1.800	3.428	27.106
B_3	-171.080	13.571	14.493	-6.280	0.000	-32.635
C_1	9.271	0.286	41.862	-0.662	2.628	35.697
C_2	- 14.062	3.133	37.728	-2.391	2.417	16.664
C_3	- 45.715	7.271	31.626	-4.840	2.088	- 5.635

a. Higher positive values are favorable for democracy or stability except for Ident. For the latter, high values are detrimental for democracy.

TABLE 16
SCHEFFE TEST ON A[a]

$$F = \frac{(\bar{X}_1 - \bar{X}_2)^2}{S_w^2 \, (n_1 + n_2) / n_1 n_2}$$

$F' = (J - 1) F_{(.01)}$

$F' = 2(4.60) = 9.200$

F scores (significant scores in boldface)

	Legit.	Ident.	Accept.	Social	No. Groups	Tolerance
$A_1 \& A_2$	0.021	0.557	0.421	0.027	**11.900**	0.365
$A_1 \& A_3$	**189.357**	**25.641**	**21.806**	**11.721**	**59.466**	**50.499**
$A_2 \& A_3$	**193.407**	**33.768**	**28.293**	**12.911**	**124.666**	**59.454**

SCHEFFE TEST ON B[a]

$F' = 2(4.60) = 9.200$

$B_1 \& B_2$	**187.801**	7.751	**12.631**	**10.865**	2.566	**30.886**
$B_1 \& B_3$	**1248.787**	**97.576**	**186.910**	**115.176**	**457.800**	**351.922**
$B_2 \& B_3$	**468.035**	**160.333**	**102.362**	**55.289**	**391.700**	**174.292**

SCHEFFE TEST ON C[a]

$F' = 2(4.60) = 9.200$

$C_1 \& C_2$	8.225	7.574	2.107	8.234	1.466	**17.690**
$C_1 \& C_3$	**45.681**	**45.598**	**12.922**	**48.085**	**9.700**	**83.426**
$C_2 \& C_3$	**15.137**	**16.002**	4.592	**16.520**	3.600	**24.283**

a. This post-hoc comparison is applied in the same manner as in Table 8.

In the results obtained for factor B, except for one measure of democracy (Ident.) and one measure of stability (No. Groups), there was a significantly greater level of development achieved by level B_1 than at level B_2. This again indicates the theoretical importance of economic values for the development of democratic stability. The two cases of nonsignificance were not expected, but their occurrence indicates that, even though a factor had a strong impact upon the dependent measures, the model was discriminating in registering effects. This gives some additional confidence that the model is useful for specifying theory implications.

The implication of the absence of significance between B_1 and B_2 for the number of groups operating within the established institutions appears to be that (especially in the light of data on Table 15), even at a moderate level of acceptance of modern economic values, there is, on the average, a basis for keeping groups satisfied with the system, a satisfaction which is not significantly improved by a higher level of acceptance. Consequently, there is little to be gained for stability in terms of the theory by enouraging a higher level of acceptance of modern economic values. A similar pattern obtains for B_1 and B_2 in relation to the other exception, the identity of source and agents of authority. Little would be gained in the level of this measure of democracy by a shift to the top level of factor B.

Factor C data indicate that political value patterns are not more closely associated with measures of democracy than with those of stability, which is contrary to expectations, especially in regard to democratic socialization of conflict. The expectation was that factor C would be especially important in shaping the outcome of this measure. It appears, however, that it is no more important than factor A and less important than factor B for this variable.

The greater impact of factor C than factor A upon tolerance was also unexpected. This would suggest in terms of the theory that higher tolerance of the system and of other groups and their demands requires much more than material payoffs from economic growth. It requires adequate acceptance levels of the more modern values such as achievement and universalism in both the economy and political subsystems which would encourage the recognition of the legitimacy of the demands of other groups and of the need for compromise in settling differences. This conclusion must be tentative, however, because the factor effects for the other measures of stability, legitimacy, and number of groups within the institutions do not uniformly support this general tendency. This is especially true of the number of groups where material payoffs appear to have a slightly greater importance than value patterns.

In regard to the three measures most directly associated with democratic development (Identification, Acceptance, Socialization), Tables 15 and 16 indicate that factor C has an effect similar to that of factors A and B on the first and last measures and the weakest effect of the three factors on Acceptance. The theoretical expectations were that factor C would have the greatest impact of the three factors on socialization of conflict, and that factors A and B would be more important for shaping the other two measures. These expectations appear to be confirmed only in the case of acceptance of democratic principles, where most apparently factor C had the least effect as compared to the other factors. In the case of identification of source and agents of authority, the results appear to be too ambiguous to confirm or disconfirm the hypothesized outcome. And in the case of socialization of conflict, the results appear to have had a greater impact on this measure, but it is clear that A effects were not greater than C effects. Despite the tentativeness of these conclusions, it is important in terms of the theory to have a clear indication that factor C is not the controlling factor for this measure as originally anticipated.

SUMMARY AND IMPLICATIONS

The preceding analyses have accomplished three things of immediate relevance. First, they have tended to confirm the validity of the models by confirming the broad-scale expectations of independent variable (factor) effects upon the dependent variables (measures). Second, they have specified in greater detail than the verbal theory several ambiguous relationships between factor and measure (and between measures) and third, they have illuminated some nonobvious or unexpected relationships which appear to be important elaborations of the modeled theories. These findings will be summarized, and some implications will be drawn from them concerning the two theories as well as for research methodology and future research possibilities.

Moore Model Summary

The following propositions of the Moore theory were supported by the simulation data analysis:

(1) In general, the balance of political power between the central government and the landed aristocracy (the degree to which one

can dominate the other) is more important for democratic development than for economic growth rates.
(2) A balance of political power produces low levels of aristocratic-bourgeois coalition potential and peasant revolt potential, and high levels of bourgeois power, rural commercialization by independent producers, and bourgeois revolution potential, all of which increase the propensity for democracy.
(3) Increases in economic development rates produce increases in the power of the bourgeoisie and the potential for bourgeois revolution and decreases in the potential for the formation of an aristocratic-bourgeois coalition.

The following propositions were clarified or specified in greater detail by the simulation data analysis:

(1) There is no correlation between bourgeois revolution potential and peasant revolution potential.
(2) The economic development rate (at any level) has no significant effect upon peasant revolt potential.
(3) The economic development rate (in general over all levels) has a greater effect upon bourgeois power development and upon the potential for an aristocratic-bourgeois coalition than upon the other three measures.
(4) The balance of political power has a greater significant effect upon rural commercialization, potential for peasant revolt, and the aristocratic-bourgeois coalition potential than upon independent bourgeois power development or bourgeois revolution potential.
(5) On the average, over all rates of economic development, levels of central government power which are below the optimum balance with the landed aristocracy are more favorable for the development of independent bourgeois power, rural commercialization by independent producers, and low aristocratic-bourgeois coalition potential than levels of central government power above the optimum balance.

The following propositions were nonobvious and illuminated by the simulation data analysis:

(1) In general, the economic development rate has no significant effect upon rural commercialization by independent producers.
(2) The highest economic development rate produces conditions favorable for development of independent bourgeois power and bourgeois revolution potential even if the political balance of power is not optimal (but is not at either extreme).

(3) A moderate rate of economic development produces conditions favorable for development of independent bourgeois power and bourgeois revolution potential if the political balance of power is optimal.
(4) On the average over all levels of political power balance, the highest rate of economic development produces a positive level of independent bourgeois power and a negative potential for aristocratic-bourgeois coalition.
(5) On the average, there is no significant difference between moderate and low rates of economic growth for bourgeois revolution potential.

Lipset Model Summary

The following propositions of the Lipset theory were supported by the simulation data analysis:

(1) In general, economic value patterns and the economic development rate are more important than political value patterns for stable democracy.
(2) If there is a similarity of levels for all three factors, higher levels for the factors produce higher values for all six measures of democratic stability.
(3) Increases in the level of modern economic value commitment and the economic development rate produce increases in legitimacy and the number of groups operating within the system. These factors are the dominant influence on the outcome of these two measures.
(4) There is a significant high positive correlation between legitimacy and democratic socialization of conflict.
(5) There is a significant high negative correlation between identification of source and agents of authority and democratic socialization of conflict.
(6) Similarity of level between economic development rate and economic value pattern and between economic value pattern and political value pattern are more important for measures of democratic stability than similarity of level between economic development rate and political value pattern.
(7) The economic development rate and economic value pattern are more important for acceptance of democratic principles than the political value pattern.

The following propositions were clarified or specified in greater detail by the simulation data analysis:

(1) There is a low positive correlation between democratic socialization of conflict and acceptance of democratic principles, number of groups operating within the system, and average group tolerance levels.
(2) Higher levels of commitment to modern political values produce greater democratic socialization of conflict, but economic values have a greater impact on variation of this measure.
(3) The rate of economic development has an impact similar to that of political values upon democratic socialization of conflict.
(4) The three factors have a very similar impact on identification of source and agents of authority.
(5) On the average over levels of the other two factors, there is no significant difference for measures of stability (except number of groups operating within the system) and measures of democracy between high and moderate rates of economic development.
(6) Of the three factors, the economic value pattern is the most important for shaping outcome of all measures, followed by economic development rate and the political value pattern, in that order.
(7) On the average over levels of the other two factors, there is no significant difference for the number of groups operating within the system and for the degree of identity of source and agents of authority between moderate and high commitment to modern economic values.

The following propositions were nonobvious and illuminated by the simulation data analysis:

(1) In general, the effect of variation in modern political value commitment was no greater for measures of democracy than for measures of stability.
(2) The political value pattern is not the dominant factor in shaping the degree of democratic socialziation of conflict.
(3) The economic value pattern is the dominant factor in shaping the degree of democratic socialization of conflict.
(4) The political value pattern is more important for variation in group tolerance than in the rate of economic development.

Implications

This summary of propositions indicates that a higher level of specification was obtained through analysis of the simulation data, thereby achieving the primary goal of elaborating in greater detail the implications of the verbal theory. The original theories each advanced propositions at a level of generality which parallels that of the propositions supported by the analyses. The second category of propositions was ambiguously dealt with by the theories or was not examined at all in terms of possibilities, although that category is not inconsistent with the major theoretical propositions. The third category of propositions contains those which the theories might imply not to be the case, and so are nonobvious or unexpected findings.

In each case, the simulation data analysis has been useful.[27] First, of the several propositions that comprise the theory, some were general and explicit in nature, and others were either tentatively advanced or implied on the basis of other statements. In the case of the former, the simulation data supported these general statements, thereby extending confidence in previous sensitivity-testing efforts to achieve a theoretically valid model.

Second, it has provided a basis for confirming, disconfirming, or withholding judgment on propositions implied by the theory under consideration. The analysis provided a basis for judging whether the tentative statements should be given serious consideration within the context of the major general propositions, and also indicated whether the implications drawn concerning subsidiary relationships were supportable or proper in terms of the major theory propositions.

Third, although the verbal theories dealt with some relationships and variables not included in the models, within the context of the patterns specifically examined by the models there are relationship possibilities not covered by the theorists or only touched upon lightly. Since model operation requires these relationships to be specified, the data generated by the simulation fill in occasional gaps in the theoretical relationship pattern of variables in a manner which relates them in a specific and coherent way to other variables and their relationships. This, together with the propositions specifying implied relationships, permits more elements of the theories to be tested. A more favorable opportunity is presented thereby for empirical validation, and this also constitutes an advance toward a better scientific explanation of democratic political development.

The range of propositions presented here should also facilitate comparative tests of the theories (as alternative or as complementary) by permitting a greater number of theory-related hypotheses to be tested. This would be beneficial in two ways. First, the greater the number of hypotheses confirmed or refuted, the greater the confidence that an accurate evaluation of the theory has been made. Second, the greater the number of hypotheses to be tested, the greater the probability that data will be available to test at least some of them. Although all the propositions explicated here are not equally important, the fact that they are all theory-related makes a test of any of them important for theory comparison and evaluation.

APPENDIX A

THE LIPSET MODEL

LIPSET MODEL FLOW CHART SYMBOL DEFINITIONS

ACC	=	Acceptance of democratic principles (Listed as Accept. in tables)
CNT(J)	=	Counts each group's operation within or without institutional framework
EFF	=	System effectiveness
GT	=	Greater than
IDEN	=	Identity of source and agent of authority (Negatively correlated with democracy) (Listed as Ident. in tables)
IN	=	Number of groups operating within institutional framework (Listed as No. Gps. in tables)
LEG	=	System legitimacy (Listed as Legit. in tables)
LT	=	Less than
NDUM	=	Dummy variable
OUT	=	Number of groups operating without institutional framework
RAND	=	Random number used for comparison (Can vary from 1 to 99)
SOC	=	Socialization of conflict (Positively correlated with democracy) (Listed as Social in tables)
STOL	=	System tolerance for group demands (Listed as Tolerance in tables)
SUM	=	Sum of group tolerance levels
THRT	=	Threat level of group demand
TOL(I)	=	Tolerance level of each group

At branch points the values derived to which the random numbers were compared were limited, for comparison purposes only, to values from 5 to 95 to prevent model operation from becoming deterministic.

A FLOW CHART INTERPRETATION OF LIPSET'S THEORY OF DEMOCRATIC POLITICAL DEVELOPMENT

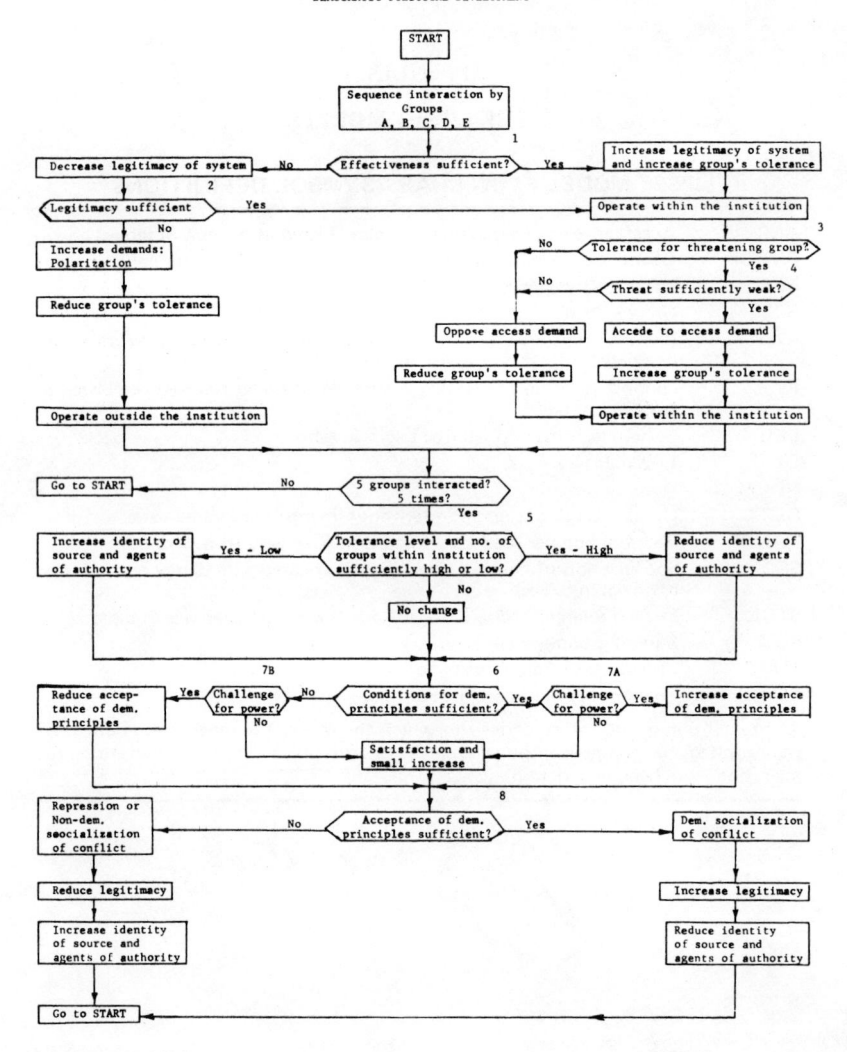

SYMBOLIC FLOW CHART MODEL OF LIPSET THEORY

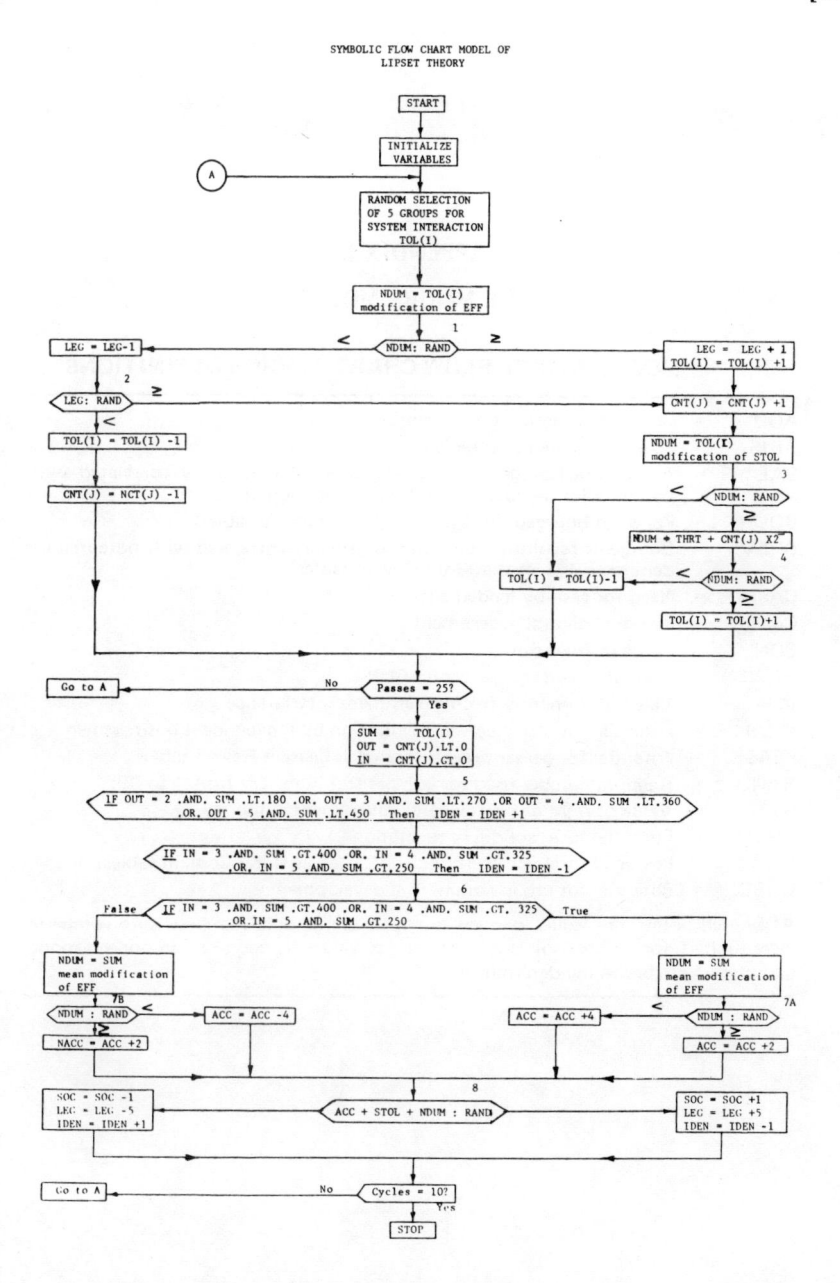

APPENDIX B

THE MOORE MODEL

MOORE MODEL FLOW CHART SYMBOL DEFINITIONS

AGD	=	Commercial agriculture potential
ARIS	=	Power of landed aristocracy
BAL	=	Aristocratic-bourgeois coalition potential (Negatively correlated with potential for democracy) (Listed as Coalition in tables)
BOUR	=	Power of bourgeoisie (Listed as Bour Power in tables)
BREV	=	Bourgeois revolution potential (Positively correlated with potential for democracy) (Listed as Bour Rev. in tables)
CASH	=	Need for cash by landed elite
CENG	=	Power of central government
CON	=	Value of free contract
GNP	=	Rate of growth of per capita GNP
IMM	=	Value of immunity from government interference
INDB	=	Potential for urban commercialization by independent businessmen
PEAS	=	Potential for peasant revolt (Listed as Peasant Rev. in tables)
RAND	=	Random number used for comparison (Can vary from 1 to 99)
RES	=	Value of right of resistance to government authority
RREV	=	Potential for reactionary revolution
RURC	=	Power of rural commercial class (Listed as Rural Com. in tables)
URBD	=	Potential for urban commercial development

At branch points the values derived to which the random numbers were compared were limited, for comparison purposes only, to values from 5 to 95 to prevent model operation from becoming deterministic.

A FLOW CHART INTERPRETATION OF MOORE'S THEORY
OF DEMOCRATIC POLITICAL DEVELOPMENT

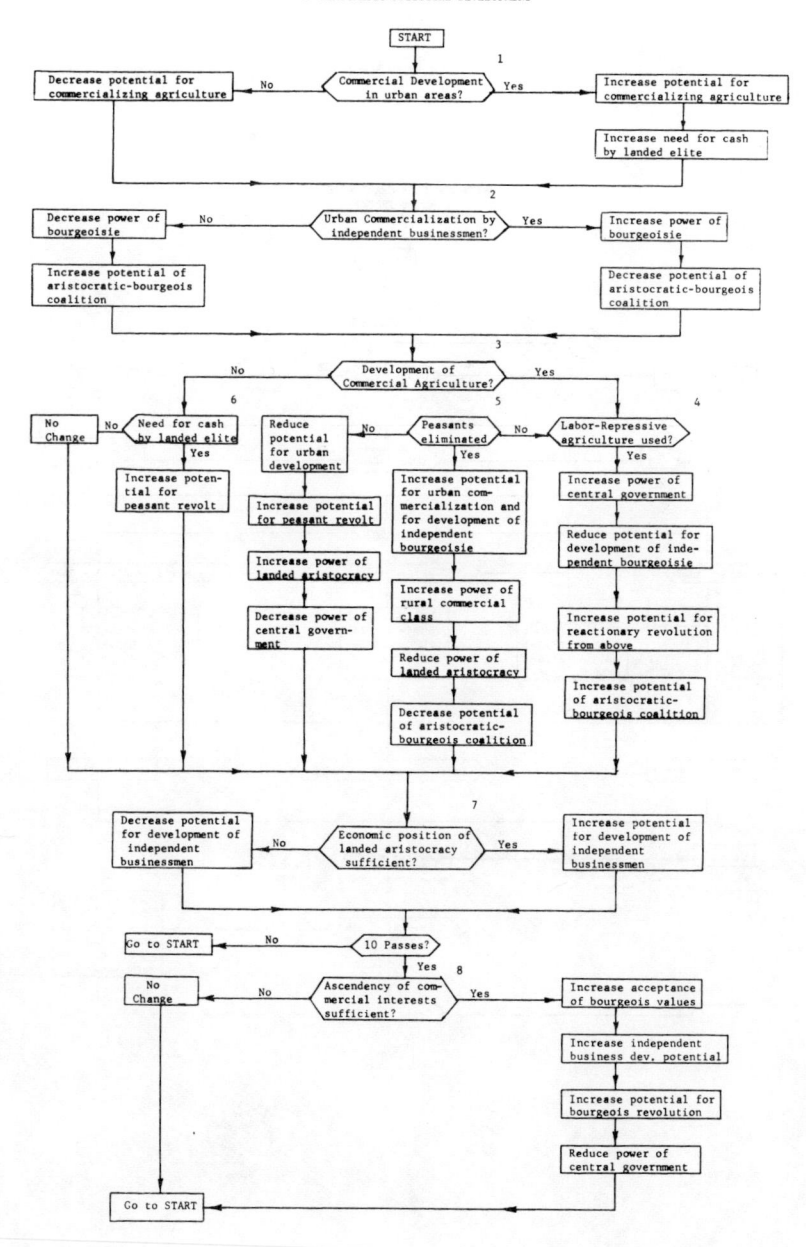

[62]

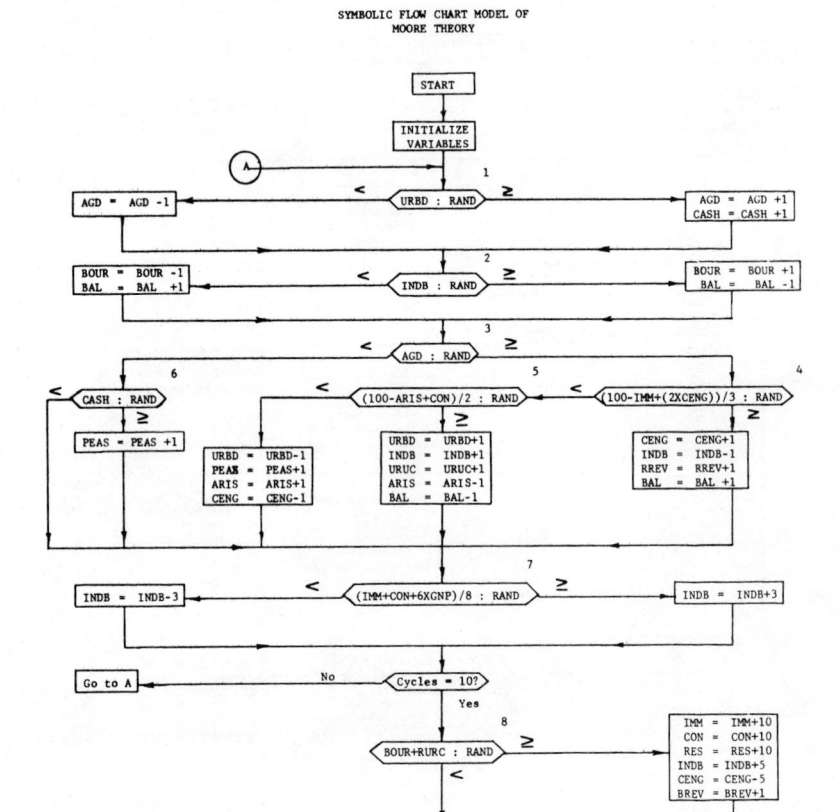

SYMBOLIC FLOW CHART MODEL OF
MOORE THEORY

```
                          START
                            │
                    INITIALIZE
                    VARIABLES
                            │
   ┌──(A)─────────────────┐ │ 1
   │                       ↓ ↓
AGD = AGD -1  ◄───<── URBD : RAND ──≥──►  AGD = AGD +1
                                          CASH = CASH +1
                            │
                            ↓ 2
BOUR = BOUR -1 ◄──<── INDB : RAND ──≥──►  BOUR = BOUR +1
BAL  = BAL  +1                            BAL  = BAL  -1
                            │
                            ↓ 3
                  <── AGD : RAND ──≥
         6        │                 │        4
    ┌────────────┤      5           │
    ↓            │                  ↓
CASH : RAND  ◄──< (100-ARIS+CON)/2 : RAND ──≥── (100-IMM+(2XCENG))/3 : RAND
    │≥                    │≥                            │≥
PEAS = PEAS+1   URBD = URBD-1    URBD = URBD+1     CENG = CENG+1
                PEAS = PEAS+1    INDB = INDB+1     INDB = INDB-1
                ARIS = ARIS+1    URUC = URUC+1     RREV = RREV+1
                CENG = CENG-1    ARIS = ARIS-1     BAL  = BAL +1
                                 BAL  = BAL -1
                            │
                            ↓ 7
INDB = INDB-3 ◄──<── (IMM+CON+6XGNP)/8 : RAND ──≥──► INDB = INDB+3
                            │
                            ↓
Go to A ◄── No ── Cycles = 10?
                     │ Yes
                     ↓ 8
                                                   IMM  = IMM+10
              BOUR+RURC : RAND ──≥──►              CON  = CON+10
                     │<                            RES  = RES+10
                     │                             INDB = INDB+5
                     │                             CENG = CENG-5
                     │                             BREV = BREV+1
                     ↓
Go to A ◄── No ── Cycles = 10?
                     │ Yes
                   STOP
```

APPENDIX C
SENSITIVITY TESTING OF THE LIPSET MODEL

Sensitivity testing involves the systematic altering of a variable or parameter, while others are held constant, to determine how sensitive the output is to the changes made. It is designed to determine which parameter settings or formulae and which variable change dimensions produce results which are acceptable in terms of the appropriate criterion, such as corresponding to empirical outcomes of the modeled phenomenon or producing the general outcomes predicted by the modeled theory. In the present case, the latter criterion was applied.

As noted by Hermann (1967: 216-231), the only relevant check on congruence between model and theory in this case is that of face validity. That is, the model is deemed valid if for given initial conditions it produces outputs which give an impression of realism in terms of the theory. This is not an error-free technique, but it appears to be the most appropriate for this type of validity check.

For the Lipset model, the primary testing of variables and parameters was done using 3 of the 27 patterns of initial conditions, the 2 extreme and the middle possibilities involving changes of all 3 independent variables. Secondary tests were made using 3 additional patterns involving change in one independent variable at a time, but using settings not identical with those used in the actual simulation runs. In this way, model operation was modified to approximate the broadly outlined predictions of the verbal theory, at least for the extreme outcomes.

The following summary lists the modification made in model operation to approximate the more obvious outcomes posited by the theory.

Branch point 4. Sensitivity testing of the model suggested this formula of using the mean of the three values. The original formula gave three times the weight to the value pattern, but model operation indicated that this did not conform to Lipset's theoretical predictions.

Branch point 4. Adding (or subtracting) one point to the threat index, as originally structured, did not have sufficient effect. Adding ten points caused an overreaction. Plus or minus two appeared to achieve adequate results.

Branch point 5. The higher settings of tolerance levels originally used as threshold levels (200, 300, 400, 500, and 450, 375, 300) biased the model too strongly in favor of identification increase. The altered levels used appeared to correct this propensity.

Branch point 7. Sensitivity testing suggested the desirability of using ±4 and ±2 rather than ±1 to allow changes in acceptance levels to have more impact on the following branch point where this level is one of three factors used.

Branch point 8. The original plan for branch point 8 made the occurrence of an insoluble problem a matter of probability related to group tolerance levels. Sensitivity testing indicated that this procedure allowed little change to occur in either direction for socialization of conflict. Consequently, branch point 8 was consolidated with its sub-branch points on the assumption that the occurrence of insoluble problems will tend to be a prevalent condition and, therefore, only a formula to determine probable outcomes is needed. This was done by giving equal weight to acceptance of democratic principles, the mean of group tolerance, and system tolerance. Sensitivity testing also indicated the need for a larger impact on legitimacy, hence the change of ±5 rather than ±1. For each occasion that branch point 8 can affect legitimacy, there is the possibility for the first part of the model to affect legitimacy by ±25, and this change at branch point 8 appeared to result in a more theoretically consistant impact on model operation output.

APPENDIX D
SENSITIVITY TESTING OF THE MOORE MODEL

As with the Lipset model, only face validity testing of congruence between model and theory was possible. Of the fifteen possible patterns of initial conditions, four were used to compare outcome with theory prediction. These patterns included the two extreme and the intermediate possibilities involving changes of both independent variables, plus one pattern involving change in one independent variable. These patterns appeared to be the most relevant for test purposes, since the theory predicts outcomes most precisely only for the extreme conditions with some indication of the impact of single variable change.

The following summary lists the changes made in model operation to approximate the more obvious outcomes posited by the theory.

Branch point 2. The possibility of a decrease in strength of the bourgeoisie was added to the original formulation to permit greater impact of varying levels of economic growth rate on this variable, which in turn affects variability of other elements of the model. This change appeared to make the effect of growth rate more consonant with the impact required by the theory.

Branch points 4 and 5. Provision was made to allow for an increase and a decrease, respectively, in the potential for an aristocratic-bourgeois coalition, thereby allowing a direct impact on this potential instead of indirect (through changes in potential for development of an independent bourgeoisie) as originally planned. This direct effect is acceptable in terms of Moore's theory and also permits this output variable to indicate outcomes that are not mere reciprocals of the strength of the bourgeoisie.

Branch point 5. Modification was made to give consideration to two other factors. First of all, in the initial formula for determining potential for peasant elimination no provision was made for the strength of the landed aristocracy. Testing of the model indicated a need for the potential to be modified by variations in this factor, a modification justified, I think, by Moore's emphasis on the importance of interests over value. This consideration is also reflected in the second factor, the addition of the possibility of relative power change between landed aristocracy and the central government. The impetus for commercialization will result in change, and, if the aristocracy is already strong, it will tend to increase its position of strength, hence a +1 increase possibility for the landed aristocracy was added. (See following paragraph for further comment on the balance of power.)

Branch point 7. Two changes were made during the testing phase. First, greater emphasis was given to GNP growth rates. Instead of treating this element as equal in importance to both values separately, it was weighted to equal three times the impact of both values combined. This change helped approximate predicted outcomes more closely as well as being justified by Moore's greater concern for material interests over values. Second, the outcome possibilities of this branch point were changed to allow still greater impact by these material considerations on potential for development of an independent business class by increasing variation levels from ±1 to ±3. A change level of ±2 did not produce satisfactory results, whereas the higher level did appear to do so for the patterns tested. Another outcome possibility was eliminated, a ±1 change in power of the central government. This possibility at branch point 7 was originally inserted only very tentatively, and when the test runs indicated an overreaction between GNP and central government strength not justified by Moore's theory, the outcome possibility was eliminated from this branch point. Instead, the −1 possibility for central government was added to the balance of power change possibility at branch point 5 which originally allowed for change only in strength of the aristocracy.

Branch point 8. Testing indicated a need for a self-reinforcing possibility for rural commercialization without labor repressive features.

Hence, an outcome possibility from this branch point was added which would reduce central government power by 5 points if the ascendency of the commercial interests was sufficient. A similar self-reinforcement for urban interests was also included by adding the option for a 5-point increase in potential for development of an independent business class. The 5-point size of change, and the 10-point increase possibility (originally one point) in the three values were needed to offset the fact that this branch point is reached only once in ten passes through the rest of the model. The potential for bourgeois revolution increase was left at +1 because this output measure, unlike the others, is not a system variable and, therefore, has no effect on the rest of the model during the simulation run.

NOTES

1. Moore (1966: 414) notes that he sees the development of a democracy "as a long and certainly incomplete struggle to do three closely related things: (1) to check arbitrary rulers, (2) to replace arbitrary rules with just and rational ones, and (3) to obtain a share for the underlying population in the making of rules." He also adds the following (1966: 429), called characteristics of the liberal and bourgeois order of society, which he equates with Western democracy: "the right to vote, representation in a legislature that makes the laws and hence is more than a rubber stamp for the executive, an objective system of law that at least in theory confers no special privileges on account of birth or inherited status, security for the rights of property and the elimination of barriers inherited from the past on its use, religious toleration, freedom of speech, and the right of peaceful assembly."

2. Lipset (1960: 27-80) notes that "Democracy in a complex society may be defined as a political system which supplies regular constitutional opportunities for changing the governing officials, and a social mechanism which permits the largest possible part of the population to influence major decisions by choosing among contenders for political office." This also "implies a number of specific conditions: (1) a 'political formula' or body of beliefs specifying which institutions—political parties, a free press, and so forth—are legitimate (accepted as proper by all); (2) one set of political leaders in office; and (3) one or more sets of recognized leaders attempting to gain office." Lipset (1963: 10, 11, 238, 239) also notes other aspects of a democracy, including rule of law, a clear distinction between source of sovereignty (legitimating factor whether a written constitution, tradition, and so on) and the agents of authority (elected officials), and protection of minority rights.

3. Kelly (1968: 74) notes limitations on this process, stating that "If certain initial conditions are present and certain hypotheses true (the programmed hypotheses), then certain conditions can be deduced for a future time (assuming no other factors operating). Computer simulation, then, can not be used to generate or confirm hypotheses. It can tell us what will happen for various possible initial conditions if the hypotheses employed are true and no variables other than those programmed are relevant."

4. The first step in this type of simulation procedure is to check internal validity of the two models by making several runs with identical values to determine if between-run variance is sufficiently small. In these and other early runs, the face validity of the simulation will also be evaluated as a gross check on how well model operation represents the modeled theory. See Hermann (1967: 216-231).

5. Tests of this kind (sensitivity tests) were performed on the two models under examination, as noted in Appendices C and D.

6. National differences can be accounted for "by indicating variations in the social development of these countries which presumably created and sustained structures carrying these values, and then 'derive' differences in their political systems which seem related in value patterns" (Lipset, 1963: 250; see also 3, 4, 343, 344, 348).

Where there are gaps in the explicit formulation of propositions or assumptions implied but not explicated, I have attempted to complete the theory by using my best judgment to make explicit the missing or vague formulations.

The development of the basic structure of the first half of the Lipset model flow chart has been guided by the efforts of Brunner (1968), who developed computer simulation models of the theories of Lipset (1960), Kautsky (1962), and Huntington (1965).

7. Lipset (1963: 103). Lipset also says elsewhere (1963: 7-8), "for the purposes of this book, I have tried to think in terms of a dynamic (that is, moving or unstable) equilibrium model, which posits that a complex society is under constant pressure to adjust its institutions to its control value systems, in order to alleviate strains created by changes in social relations; and which asserts that the failure to do so results in political disturbance."

8. In the model to be developed, legitimacy and tolerance are dependent variables used as two indicators of stability. Lipset does not define stability explicitly, mentioning only the institutionalizing of a democratic process (Lipset's definition of democracy was noted above) and its persistence over time (Lipset, 1963: 364 and throughout).

9. Lipset (1963: 237, 250, 268, 289). Lipset bases his analysis upon an examination of nations that have a similar religious background. They are considered democratic, but some are stable (United States, Britain, Canada, Australia) while two are unstable (France and Germany). The choice of historical focus and end state to be explained present some analytic differences between Lipset and Moore. For example, Lipset attempts to evaluate post-World War II democracy in West Germany in terms of its value patterns and concludes that it is not yet institutionalized enough to be termed stable. Barrington Moore, Jr., on the other hand (as noted previously), examines the pattern of economic and social development of Germany, which he sees producing the reactionary political system of Nazi Germany. Moore views post-World War II developments in West German politics as being determined essentially by international political and military intervention rather than by domestic changes, hence not explainable by his propositions concerning indigenous change. Moore attempts to explain (by examining indigenous variables) why democratic government tends to emerge given certain conditions (even if the system is unstable, as Lipset concludes in the case of France), whereas Lipset attempts to explain why a democratic form of government tends to develop stability, however initiated. These considerations again indicate the limited nature of these theoretical efforts in terms of range of factors considered.

10. Lipset (1963: 43) speaks of leaders in new states "who view criticism of themselves as tantamount to an attack on the nation itself. Such behavior characterizes leaders of polities in which the concept of democratic succession to office has not been institutionalized." A two-party system also aids this process because "the 'out' party can always realistically aspire to gain office within a few years" (1963: 307).

11. The value pattern variables used by Lipset appear to be useful for political analysis. The first three continua have been used, at least implicitly, by theorists for centuries. The achievement-ascription pattern is important for the type of legitimating factor that is acceptable for political leaders (an achievement orientation being important for accepting popular election as legitimizing). The equalitarianism-elitism pattern relates to suffrage rights and to representative government. And the universalism-particularism pattern is important for concepts such as equality before the law. Lipset's use of these value patterns as continua rather than as polarities or ideal types allows him to examine trends and tendencies of a system which may

exhibit a mixed pattern. Because of their generality, the use of value patterns will not permit one to explain or predict individual events, but they appear to be relevant to a better understanding of a long-term historical process (Lipset, 1963: 209-211).

12. Although there are no obvious demarcations among low, medium, and high rates of growth, these percentage variations in growth rates do appear in the empirical world. It does not appear unjustified, therefore, to use this range of variation to operationalize the propositions stated. See, for example, Adelman (1961: 4) and Villard (1963: 197-198). The absolute levels of growth do not appear to be as important, however, as the fact that the scale gives us a range of variability that indicates the relative importance of different rates of growth when related to achievement levels to form the initial effectiveness level.

13. This application is guided by the propositions noted previously that if achievement levels are high, growth rates should also be high; and, conversely, if achievement levels are low, then growth rates should also be low so as not to be disruptive. It also attempts to account for the assumption that low achievement levels and low growth rates are not conducive to the maintenance or improvement of legitimacy of a newly democratic political system.

14. Random numbers are used at each branch point because the complexity of the modeled theory is such that with present levels of knowledge it is not possible to design an optimum mode of operation for the model within defined and unvarying conditions. Such a model would be deterministic. As McMillan and Gonzalez (1968: 13-14) note, "More typically, systems are characterized by attributes that take values which are the result of factors whose interaction is at best poorly understood. These attributes or variables are 'produced' by successive trials of stochastic processes. Such processes are described as repetitions of 'experiments' whose results are probabilistic —i.e., determined by chance." The random number comparison procedure used in the Lipset and Moore models is the stochastic process which makes them probabilistic rather than deterministic models.

15. Lipset (1963: 210). This is especially true, Lipset notes, of universalism and achievement values (1963: 268).

16. Moore (1966: xvii). He also notes that the book "is an attempt to discover the range of historical conditions under which either or both of these rural groups have become important forces behind the emergence of Western parliamentary versions of democracy, and dictatorships of the right and the left, that is fascist and communist regimes" (1966: xi).

17. In addition, democracy implies the right to vote, a representative legislature, an objective system of law, religious toleration, freedom of speech, and the right to peaceful assembly (1966: 429).

18. A crucial independent variable (discussed below and in the next section) is the balance of political power between the central government and the landed aristocracy. If there is equality between these two elements, there is (in regard to this variable) an optimum chance for the development of conditions favorable for democracy such as the emergence of a strong land-owning and operating commercial class and an urban commercial class. Russett (1964) found a positive relationship between equality of land distribution and stable democracy, based upon comparison between nations at a recent point in time. Moore's conception of owner-operator in agriculture assumes a reduction in ownership inequality, but this is a dependent variable for him. He attempts to explain why the inequality persists or diminishes over time within individual countries. In doing so, he moves one step deeper into the

empirical explanation process and uses an analytic approach (longitudinal rather than cross-sectional) that is more directly relevant to developmental analysis.

19. The Moore model data are analyzed first because this model is the less complex of the two, and it will enable the reader unfamiliar with this form of analysis to comprehend more easily the concepts and tests employed in the evaluation.

20. The MANOVA and ANOVA data are derived from a computer programmed analysis designed by the Biometric Laboratory of the University of Miami (Florida) and applied by the Behavioral Sciences Laboratory of Ohio State University. For reference on univariate ANOVA, see Hays (1963) and Ferguson (1966). For reference on multivariate ANOVA, see Morrison (1967: 173-180).

21. The absence of a strong AB interaction effect increases the interpretability of the main effects. A significant interaction tends to restrict the main effect.

22. For a brief discussion of this post-hoc test, see Ferguson (1966: 296-297) and Hays (1963: 483-485).

23. It appears unlikely that the rural commercialization measure could be significantly affected at the 0.01 level, as indicated by the univariate F test, and not have at least one significant difference displayed by the Scheffé post-hoc comparison test. But the Scheffé test was rechecked and confirmed for this measure. It could be noted, however, that the A_1 and A_3 comparison comes very close to achieving a significant score, especially when compared to the scores for peasant revolution which obtained a nonsignificant univariate F test result of 0.71.

24. Perhaps a more powerful post-hoc test, such as the Duncan Multiple Range Test could have been used to discriminate factor effects. But the Scheffé test was chosen because it has the same power as the univariate F test, and was considered sufficient for present purposes.

25. An analysis program similar to that used for the Moore model data was used for these data.

26. It is interesting to note in Table 15 that A_2, the moderate rate of growth, produced values for all six measures which indicated a higher propensity for political stability and democracy than did A_1, the highest rate of growth, although the Scheffé test indicates that the difference is not significant.

27. Kelly (1968: 74) notes that "computer simulation, then, can not be used to generate or confirm hypotheses. It can tell us what will happen for various possible initial conditions if the hypotheses employed are true and no variables other than those programmed are relevant." The present project does not contradict these statements by Kelly since the propositions (or hypotheses) generated were implications derivable from the modeled theory, and the support given to propositions is not empirical confirmation but additional confirmation that the model conforms to the theory. Whether or not the hypotheses derived from the theories are empirically confirmed is a separate research problem, discussed briefly below.

REFERENCES

ADELMAN, I. (1961) Theories of Economic Growth and Development. Palo Alto, Calif.: Stanford Univ. Press.

ALMOND, G. A. and G. B. POWELL (1966) Comparative Politics: A Developmental Approach. Boston: Little, Brown.

ANDERSON, T. W. (1958) Introduction to Multivariate Statistical Analysis. New York: John Wiley.

APTER, D. (1965) The Politics of Modernization. Chicago: Univ. of Chicago Press.

BRUNNER, R. D. (1968) "Some comments on simulating theories of political development," pp. 329-342 in W. D. Coplin (ed.) Simulation in the Study of Politics. Chicago: Markham.

CUTRIGHT, P. (1963) "National political development: its measurement and social correlates," pp. 569-582 in N. W. Polsby et al. (eds.) Politics and Social Life. Boston: Houghton Mifflin.

DAWSON, R. (1962) "Simulation in the social sciences," pp. 1-15 in H. Guetzkow (ed.) Simulation in the Social Sciences. Englewood Cliffs, N.J.: Prentice-Hall.

DEUTSCH, K. W. (1961) "Social mobilization and political development." Amer. Pol. Sci. Rev. 55 (September): 493-514.

EISENSTADT, S. N. (1966) Modernization: Protest and Change. Englewood Cliffs, N.J.: Prentice-Hall.

--- (1964) "Modernization growth and diversity." India Q. 20 (January, March): 18-42.

EMERSON, R. (1964) From Empire to Nation. Boston: Beacon.

EVANS, G. W. II, G. F. WALLACE, and G. L. SUTHERLAND (1967) Simulation Using Digital Computers. Englewood Cliffs, N.J.: Prentice-Hall.

FERGUSON, G. A. (1966) Statistical Analysis in Psychology and Education. New York: McGraw-Hill.

FIELD, G. L. (1967) Comparative Political Development. Ithaca, N.Y.: Cornell Univ. Press.

FRIJDA, N. H. (1967) "Problems of computer simulation." Behavioral Sci. 12 (January): 59-67.

HAYS, W. L. (1963) Statistics. New York: Holt, Rinehart & Winston.

HERMANN, C. F. (1967) "Validation problems in games and simulations with special reference to models of international politics." Behavioral Sci. 12 (May): 216-231.

HOLLAND, E. P. and R. W. GILLESPIE (1963) Experiments on a Simulated Underdeveloped Economy. Cambridge, Mass.: MIT Press.

HUNTINGTON, S. P. (1965) "Political development and political decay." World Politics 17 (January): 386-430.

KAUTSKY, J. H. (1962) Political Change in Underdeveloped Countries: Nationalism and Communism. New York: John Wiley.

KELLY, E. W. (1968) "Technique of studying coalition formation." Midwest J. of Pol. Sci. 19 (February): 62-84.

LERNER, D. (1958) The Passing of Traditional Society. Glencoe: Free Press.

LIPSET, S. M. (1963) The First New Nation. New York: Basic Books.

---(1960) Political Man. Garden City, N.Y.: Doubleday.

MacIVER, R. M. (1947) The Web of Government. New York: Macmillan.

--- (1926) The Modern State. New York: Oxford Univ. Press.

McMILLAN, C. and R. F. GONZALEZ (1968) A Computer Approach to Decision Models. Homewood, Ill.: Richard D. Irwin.

MEEHAN, E. L. (1965) The Theory and Method of Political Analysis. Homewood, Ill.: Dorsey.

MILL, J. S. (1958) Considerations on Representative Government. Indianapolis: Bobbs-Merrill.

MOORE, B., Jr. (1966) Social Origins of Dictatorship and Democracy: Lord and Peasant in the Making of the Modern World. Boston: Beacon.

MORRISON, D. F. (1967) Multivariate Statistical Methods. New York: McGraw-Hill.

NEUBAUER, D. E. (1967) "Some conditions of democracy." Amer. Pol. Sci. Rev. 61 (December): 1002-1009.

PYE, L. (1966) Aspects of Political Development. Boston: Little, Brown.

--- (1964) Politics, Personality and Nation Building. New Haven, Conn.: Yale Univ. Press.

RUSSETT, B. M. (1964) "Inequality and instability: the relation of land tenure to politics." World Politics 16 (April): 442-454.

SCOTT, A. M., with W. A. LUCAS and T. M. LUCAS (1966) Simulation and National Development. New York: John Wiley.

SHILS, E. (19   ton.
VERBA, S. (s." World
Politics 16

VILLARD, H. H. (1963) Economic Development. New York: Holt, Rinehart & Winston.

ZELDITCH, M., Jr., and W. M. EVANS (1962) "Simulated bureaucracies: a methodological analysis," pp. 48-60 in H. Guetzkow (ed.) Simulation in the Social Sciences: Readings. Englewood Cliffs, N.J.: Prentice-Hall.

ROLAND F. MOY is assistant professor, Department of Political Science, at Appalachian State University. His specialty is comparative political development and normative theory, and his research interests, in addition to international politics, involve the application of quantitative methods to normative problems arising in national political change. He holds M.A. and Ph.D. degrees from The Ohio State University.